306·89   8.99.

This book is to be returned on or before
the last date stamped below.

**AYLESBURY COLLEGE
LIBRARY**

This book may be renewed by personal application, post
or telephone, quoting date, author and title.

LIBREX

Caught in the Middle

Helping children to cope with
separation and divorce

ANNE CHARLISH

Consultants:
Monica Cockett and Dr John Tripp

WARD LOCK

A WARD LOCK BOOK

First published in the UK 1997
by Ward Lock
Wellington House
125 Strand
LONDON
WC2R 0BB

A Cassell Imprint

Distributed in the United States
by Sterling Publishing Co., Inc.
387 Park Avenue South, New York, NY 10016-8810

A British Library Cataloguing in Publication
Data block for this book may be obtained from
the British Library

ISBN 0 7063 7456 8
Typeset by Business Color Print Ltd
Printed and bound in Great Britain by Biddles Ltd

Contents

For Roger and Graham

Note

The non-resident parent is nearly always referred to as 'he', as this reflects the norm for the majority. The non-resident parent may equally be the mother.

The author and contributors

The author

Anne Charlish is a respected health and medical writer and broadcaster. She is the author of over twenty books on subjects ranging from smoking and schizophrenia to pregnancy. In 1993 she won the Medical Journalists' Association Pain Relief Award for *The Complete Arthritis Handbook*. She also contributes regularly to a wide range of magazines, including *Good Housekeeping*, *Essentials* and *Health and Fitness*.

The contributors

Monica Cockett is a research fellow at the Department of Child Health, Postgraduate Medical School, University of Exeter. She has worked as a researcher there for the past twelve years and has a background in social policy and child care. Her work during the past eight years has included research into families, children and divorce and evaluating mediation services set up locally to support divorcing families. She has also been involved locally and nationally in the management training and supervision of mediation practice. She is concerned with the promotion of good professional mediation services nationwide.

Dr John Tripp attracted worldwide media attention in 1994 when BBC Television aired a special *Panorama* programme devoted to his research on the effects of divorce upon children. He is a consultant paediatrician at the Royal Devon and Exeter Hospital and also a senior lecturer in Child Health at the Postgraduate Medical School,

University of Exeter. His research interests have led him into broader areas of child health, including disability, family breakdown and teenage sexuality, in addition to continuing clinical and physiological research. For many years Dr Tripp has been a member of the Royal College of Physicians' Committee on Ethical Issues in Medicine.

Acknowledgements

I would like to thank Angus for his support, encouragement, wit and, not least, his skills in the kitchen during the writing of this book.

I am also indebted to Helen Denholm, a distinguished and committed editor, with whom it has been a pleasure to work.

Anne Charlish

The author and publisher gratefully acknowledge permission to quote from the following books:

The Divorce Handbook, Fiona Shackleton and Olivia Timbs (Thorsons, 1992)

The Spirit of the Community, Amitai Etzioni (Fontana Press, 1995)

Surviving the Breakup: How Children and Parents Cope with Divorce, Judith Wallerstein and Joan Berlin Kelly. This book was originally published in 1980 by Grant McIntyre in London and BasicBooks in New York. Quoted by permission of HarperCollins Publishers, Inc., New York and Blackwell Publishers, Oxford

Every effort has been made to trace the copyright holder of *Splitting Up* by Catherine Itzin, but we have been unable to do so. The publishers will be pleased to hear from the copyright holder so that this omission can be rectified.

Introduction

For one in three children under the age of sixteen, experience of family life in the late 1990s will include the breakdown of their parents' relationship. It may also include living in a single-parent family for a part of their childhood, from which they may progress into a stepfamily. Second marriages may be even less secure for children, as one in two is currently likely to break down. Children and parents can no longer rely on a single experience or definition of 'family'.

The uncomfortable message that children do not feel as positive about family reorganization as perhaps their parents do is not a surprising one and is becoming increasingly difficult to ignore.

The importance of listening to children is emphasized by the legislation, in the form of the Children Act 1989, which now governs any legal dealings with families and children. The United Nations Charter on the Rights of the Child, implemented in nine countries in 1989, states very clearly for the first time that the child has a right to be heard, and to have access to both parents whenever possible. We need to provide support for parents in their difficult task of bringing up children in a social environment that appears increasingly hostile to families.

Obtaining and keeping a job and providing a family home are often no longer the obvious or attainable options. While many men now find themselves unemployed, there is an increase in low-paid or part-time work for women, so that the traditional roles within the family have needed adjustment.

In the past thirty years these changing attitudes to families and parenthood have made permanence and life-long commitment more difficult to establish and sustain. Marriage, once seen as *the*

1

most important transitition to adulthood, is now viewed with some scepticism by a growing number of young people. Cohabitation is now much more common and increasingly involves children. One-third of all children born in 1994 were born to parents who were not married to each other.

The parents

The publication *Marital Breakdown and the Health of the Nation* (1995), a review of the abundant evidence of the effects of family breakdown, clearly outlines the fact that children and parents can suffer health and social problems. Separated mothers and fathers are more likely to visit their doctor or to have a stress-related illness that leads to hospital admission. Married people smoke and drink less than the divorced and are less likely to be absent from work for family reasons. Although high-risk sexual behaviour is traditionally associated with young people, divorced men are more likely to practise unsafe sex.

Women try harder to save relationships, but once they have decided that there is no chance for improvement, they are more likely to seek a divorce than their partners. More men (51 per cent) than women (29 per cent), once they have divorced, regret their decision to do so. Of even greater concern, perhaps, is the increasing number of young men represented in the annual suicide statistics, with research evidence showing that a reduced role within the family may be a contributory factor.

The parent with care of the children

Children's security is dependent on how well their resident parent manages to carry on with life in new circumstances. Even those who are happy to be free of the old relationship can find the responsibility of looking after the children harder than they expected.

A study carried out in the USA recently showed that, one year after separation, most women and children were living on half their previous income. There is usually less money for everyone. Women with the primary care of children may have to find a job, which, coupled with extra child-care responsibilities, can be very tiring and makes parenting even more stressful.

If parents do not form a new long-term relationship following separation, many will have several shorter relationships, which can seem very threatening to a child who is already experiencing diminished parental attention.

The non-resident parent

As already indicated, many of these parents (mostly fathers) later regret their divorce. The loss of contact, involvement and shared responsibility for their children are sources of much distress. A number will live, at least for a time, in accommodation to which it is not possible to bring their children (especially teenage girls) for overnight visits. This makes contact more difficult to organize.

The children

It has been known for some time from the results of the large national birth cohort studies, in the UK and elsewhere (such as M.E.J. Wadsworth's *The Imprint of Time. Childhood History and Adult Life*), that there are both long- and short-term disadvantages for children following parental separation; more recent research, in the form of the Exeter Family Study, tells the same story.

The basic fact is that parental separation exposes children to a range of risk factors, some of which they manage to deal with, and some of which threaten to overwhelm them. Parents are the best placed, yet not always best prepared, to help their children overcome these difficulties and start a new life.

What are the problems?

Children, on the whole, have to live with the decisions that adults make for them about their life. If one or both parents decide that they can no longer stay together, or the relationship becomes impossible because of violence, cruelty or abuse, the child has little power to alter or influence the events that follow. To a child the decision of one parent to leave can seem as if the parent has chosen between the child and a new life. Kalter, an American psychologist, has outlined very clearly the main problems that children have to deal with after their parents part ('Predictors of Children's Post-divorce Adjustment' in *American Journal of Orthopsychiatry* 59, 605–20. 1989). These include:

▪ the loss or partial loss of relationship with the non-resident parent.

▪ changed relationship with the parent with whom the child lives (with care).

▪ interparental conflict.

▪ economic distress.

▪ the degree of adaptation by the parent with care to changed life circumstances.

▪ remarriage of either parent.

How can the problems be tackled?

In the face of this bleak perspective, one of the positive results of discovering and defining problems is to throw some light on how to deal with them. Research has indicated several important ways of providing support for children and assisting their adaptation to family change (M. Rutter and D. Smith, eds, 'Psychosocial Disorders in Young People', *Time Trends and Their Causes*, 1995).

The Family Law Bill, which may, by the time of publication of this book, be on the statute book, has made important changes to the way that parents end their marriages. Although parents and children flourish best in harmonious homes, in reality this is not always possible to achieve or maintain. The emphasis is placed on helping both parents, whether or not they choose to end the relationship, to co-operate with each other after separation for the sake of their children. This can be very difficult, but in the light of such strong evidence that children can adapt more easily if parents are able to communicate with each other, parents need every encouragement to do so.

Good self-esteem

It is no surprise that children who feel good about themselves, with confidence in their ability to achieve, will be able to approach their school and social lives with more equanimity than those who feel miserable, sad or guilty. Helping children develop and maintain confidence in themselves is assisted by a stable environment and good supportive relationships with parents and other important adults. Doing well at school and receiving recognition for this are also very important to children. When parents separate, they face the challenge of providing this for their children often in less than favourable circumstances.

Changes in children's lives

Although some things will inevitably have to change in children's lives when families separate, if parents can keep these to a minimum it gives children a chance to 'recover their balance'. Staying in the family home or, if a move is inevitable, in the same locality, at least for the first year or two, although not always financially possible, does help to reduce the chances of a whole cycle of other changes. Children can usually continue at the same school, see the same friends and maintain their neighbourhood links.

Keeping in touch

The most painful problem for parents, and the most vital one to sort out for children, is how to maintain good contact arrangements when feelings between parents are often strongly negative. It is important to emphasize the parent role rather than the partner role, and to understand that the child's view of each parent will differ from the parental perspective. Remembering that two parents are better than one in terms of shared financial and emotional responsibility can help to ease the arrangements.

A sad corollary to lessened contact with a parent is that the child may also lose touch with grandparents and other relatives, who will usually have been an emotional support. Anger between parents can spill over into the extended family, and family friends who may divide themselves into two separate camps and are thus less useful to the child.

Providing explanations

Children may feel very confused and kept in the dark about changes that have to be made. These feelings of insecurity, often exacerbated by self-blame, can be eased by talking to children and involving them in some of the day-to-day decisions, while protecting them from the major decision-making processes, which should rightly remain between adults. Reassurance that parents are endeavouring to work together frees children from having to weigh up one view against another. This is sometimes very difficult for parents to do, but children find it very painful to share their time between parents who can no longer speak to each other.

Remarriage, repartnering

Most parents hope that, following the end of one relationship, they will be able to form another, which this time will be more successful. When the initial stages of disentanglement are over, although some parents will view themselves as entirely blameless for the failure of their relationship, many will be able to take a more measured view and accept their own share of responsibility. This is a very important requisite for trying to achieve a successful second relationship, which is statistically more risky than a first marriage.

Second relationships are inevitably more complicated, and for children the competition for attention that new partners and new siblings present can often seem very daunting. The research evidence is not very encouraging, as children of stepfamilies are more likely to leave home earlier and have earlier, more problematic relationships themselves, which expose them to the dangers of repeating the cycle. The loss of one parent from the home and the replacement by a new parental figure provide a conflict of loyalties which may never be resolved. Parents, in their new-found happiness, sometimes overlook the fact that their children may not share their enthusiasm for the new partner. Concentrating on making sure that children do not have too much of a struggle to engage their parent's attention, and providing the opportunity for continuing a good relationship with both parents, form central planks for children's survival in a second relationship/marriage. A concerted attempt on the part of parents to explain and share views and feelings has been shown from research to assist children to settle more comfortably into what is often for them an alien family environment.

Caught in the Middle

This book is by an author with a great deal of experience in writing about technical subjects for a lay readership. Anne Charlish describes the many complex situations and issues that parents face in relation to separation. By liberal use of quotations the message is brought very much alive. Material from an extensive range of research monographs, reviews and publications has been distilled and interpreted in a thoroughly readable and practical narrative. Checklists and didactic advice offer resources for parents to use but clearly need to be used and interpreted within the context of the enormous variations between the circumstances and resources of individuals, couples, parents and children.

We strongly support the aims of this book to highlight the problems parents may encounter and to suggest ways in which they can seek and find solutions to some of their everyday problems. Family doctors, family lawyers and children's teachers are frequently quoted by parents as being helpful and understanding when family breakdown occurs. Organizations such as Relate offer assistance with relationship problems. The Citizen's Advice Bureau can provide advice and information about local initiatives and financial matters. Mediation services, found in many towns and cities, work alongside family lawyers to create a conciliatory approach to post-separation arrangements.

In acting as consultants to the book, we have been concerned that parents will understand the legal and emotional complexities of family breakdown. The presentation and interpretation of the subject matter are the responsibility of the author, who offers her own particular views and advice to parents. It is hoped that parents will gain courage from the information and the interpretation of research, and from practical suggestion for parenting in changed family circumstances.

Children have to live within the world created for them by others. The quality of their future lives as parents and partners depends on the provision of a positive rather than a negative blueprint of family life to carry with them into adulthood.

Monica Cockett
John Tripp

1 Trouble at home

'It's like having a stranger in the house. We don't communicate, we no longer look at one another. We don't laugh. I feel anxious and emotionally drained most of the time. And, of course, the children pick up on things: they play me up all the time and bicker and squabble endlessly between themselves. I'd like to get something sorted out, if only for their sakes.'

The breakdown of a marriage is a major trauma for everyone. Marital breakdown is second only to bereavement among the causes of stress for adults. The death of a spouse registers 100 units in the most widely used scale (formulated by two American researchers, Thomas Holmes and Richard Rahe, in 1967), while divorce represents 73 units and marital separation 65 units. The process of divorce typically comprises a number of recognized causes of stress – for example, moving house, trouble with in-laws, change in living conditions and change of children's schools.

Taken together, the stress endured by those in a failing marriage can pose a significant health risk to husband and to wife and to their children. If you experience between 150 and 300 units within a two-year period, you have a 50 per cent chance of a serious change in your health within the next twelve months. A rating of over 300 units increases your chances of impaired health to 80 per cent.

How do you know that your marriage is in trouble?

A troubled relationship bears certain quickly recognizable characteristics, which include emotional withdrawal, negative outlook and attitudes, secretiveness, detachment, irritability, unexplained explosive rages, lack of close eye contact and physical contact, a marked and significant change in attitudes and behaviour, physical or verbal abuse, self-destructive behaviour (over- or under-eating, drinking to excess, gambling, accruing substantial debts), depression, problems with the children and a sense, above all, of having lost your best friend and partner.

Do any of these signs of problems within a marriage relate to you? Healthy marriages may show a few of these features, but several of them suggests there is a problem:

- You no longer feel happy and at ease with your partner.

- You no longer regard your partner as your closest friend.

- Making love has neither the frequency nor the intensity it used to have (sex is often the first thing to go in an ailing relationship).

- An incompatibility of sex drive exists between you and your partner.

- You no longer communicate effectively with each other.

- There is a lack of respect between you.

- There is a lack of trust between you.

- You argue all the time.

- One partner is distanced, detached, apparently no longer part of a couple.

- There is a hardening of attitudes so that one or both refuses to discuss, negotiate or compromise.

- The factor that attracted you most when you met your partner is now the thing that you find the most irritating.

▨ One or both partners is not functioning fully – perhaps they are unable or unwilling to work, unable or unwilling to make love or unable or unwilling to socialize with friends.

▨ One partner appears to the other to be dependent upon them for their wellbeing

What makes a good marriage? A good marriage depends upon a good degree of stability, the one factor that outweighs everything else. This is not to say that an unstable marriage is necessarily a bad one, simply that such a marriage is more likely to cause each partner stress and that it is more likely to collapse under the pressure of external stresses.

What makes for stability within marriage? Psychologists who specialize in love, sex and marital relationships have defined the similarities between partners, and the differences, that improve the potential for compatibility and thus stability:

▨ Willingness to play your gender role. It may surprise readers that research shows that a relationship is more likely to endure if the man conforms with his gender role and shows more of the male qualities than the female, with the female possessing more of the feminine qualities than her partner. If the man is more neurotic than his wife, problems may result. Equally, if the woman is more 'macho' and more bombastic than her partner, difficulties may arise.

▨ Although feminists will not like this, much research evidence shows that relationships founded on traditional roles are more stable than others. A marriage in which the woman is the main breadwinner, for example, is much more likely to break down than one in which the man takes that role.

▨ Verbal communication is a fundamental need for most women: many men find this irritating. If verbal communication is harmonized to suit both partners, the marriage is more stable.

- Closeness in age. Research has shown that women tend to be happiest when their partner is about two years older than they are.

- Shared race.

- Shared religion (or absence of religion in both family backgrounds).

- Shared social class.

- Shared intelligence and education.

- Shared interests and profession.

- Similar social and political beliefs and general attitude to life.

- If the woman is slightly more verbally extrovert than her partner, the relationship will be more stable than if the male is the more talkative of the two.

- What about 'opposites attract'? It works if the male is more intelligent, earns more or exhibits very male characteristics. The partnership is unstable, however, if the man is less intelligent, earns less or exhibits feminine qualities. It is considered potentially stable if the woman is bubbly and he is on the quiet side, but less so if the characteristics are reversed.

- Willingness on the part of both partners to negotiate and compromise.

- Compatible sex drive between the pair.

Avoiding divorce

It is, of course, vitally important for you and your children to be able to recognize the warning signs of a marriage in trouble. Much unhappiness and some divorces could be avoided altogether if both partners were able and willing to take constructive steps before the point is reached where the relationship has deteriorated so badly that divorce becomes inevitable.

Most couples experience bad patches in their marriage, when arguing or a silent detachment appears to be the main activity. Many survive these patches and succeed in resolving issues. It is those who do not resolve the issues who may falter. In the absence of real issues, about which the partners genuinely and profoundly disagree, some couples may find that they argue as a matter of course about all sorts of mundane and trivial matters. This does not augur well for a happy, lasting marriage.

People who have been brought up in an argumentative family often find themselves within argumentative marriages. They have become accustomed to functioning in an argumentative, confrontational way: that is simply their style. They may not be expressing real conflicts or real anger and would be surprised to learn that other less argumentative friends regarded their marriage as being in danger.

Some people heartily dislike the argumentative style and would prefer peace at almost any cost. A marriage in which one partner is peace-loving and the other is confrontational is bound to run into problems from time to time. It would be worth determining, perhaps with the help of a marriage guidance counsellor, what lies at the root of your arguments. Are there issues that can be resolved? Do you argue simply because it is in both your natures? Are you arguing because of profound, unvoiced conflicts? Do you feel that your partner has changed since you married? Have you yourself or your own work/lifestyle changed? A counsellor can help you to discover the answers to these questions for yourself. It would be better if both you and your partner visited the counsellor, but it is not essential. You will still benefit by visiting a counsellor alone, if that is necessary.

We all hope, ideally, to be able to regard home as a harmonious haven, a sanctuary from the outside world. Once a marriage has become a battleground, home no longer extends the welcome it once did. Some will desert the marriage in search of peace, and it is therefore important to seek to bring continual arguments to a close before the marriage has become so undermined that it cannot continue. Most people argue, and that is psychologically healthy, but not to the exclusion of almost everything else.

'Mum was always crying and Dad was always shouting at her,' says the son of now-divorced parents. 'But when he went to live in a different place and came to visit us he was much nicer. I don't know why he wasn't like that when he lived with us.'

Divorce does sometimes become the next logical step. It is a step, however, that should be taken with the utmost caution. This is not to say that we should try to turn the clock back, for the sake of our children, and avoid divorce at all costs. But it is vital that divorce is never undertaken in a spirit of revenge, for example. It should be contemplated only when the marriage has finally and irretrievably collapsed. Divorce only seldom produces a solution with which all parties are content. Many women and many men regret their divorce, often coming to see that it could have been avoided.

'We weren't getting on particularly well,' remembers a divorced mother of three children. 'My husband's job entailed very long hours, so we didn't see much of him. Even at weekends, he'd have work to do, or a conference to go to. Quite frankly, I thought I'd be better off without him. But I didn't realize just how much quiet background support he brought to us as a family. He was completely devastated when I told him I wanted a divorce. He couldn't even begin to understand. He simply thought that he had been doing what was expected of him – being the breadwinner – and that was it. Now, of course, I miss him . . . and I know the children blame me bitterly for breaking up the family. My husband has remarried now, and I live in fear of the children telling me one day that they want to go and live with their father and his new wife.'

A father of two boys recalls:

'I had been married, quite happily I thought, for about six years. There was a researcher in my department who used to come to me for guidance and advice about her work. We were both due to attend a conference one weekend and she asked me for a lift. We got talking, naturally – and all of a sudden she said, quite simply, "If you weren't married, I'd marry you tomorrow." It really all started from there. I looked at her in quite a new light. I told my wife that I had fallen in love with someone else, because I did not want to lie to her. She said, and I'll never forgive her for this, "Not under my roof, you don't," and she chucked me out. The affair started then. I used to see the children every day and then go back to my flat. Sue, the researcher, found my pain and anger with the marital breakup very difficult to cope with. She made increasing demands on me. She wanted me to convert to Judaism, she wanted me to come abroad with her to work: she seemed completely to overlook the fact that I had two small sons with whom I wanted close and regular contact. The whole thing was a disaster from start to finish. She kept refusing to see me because I was so upset. I kept returning to my wife, trying to make a fresh start . . . and then Sue would contact me, telling me that she could not bear to be apart from me. I went back and forth like this for over a year. In the end my wife took up with an old schoolfriend of mine, which caused me a lot of pain. Divorce simply became inevitable, but I will regret for the rest of my days having left my boys.'

Very few children of divorcing parents welcome the breakup: the great majority of children would prefer to see their parents together even if the family atmosphere is difficult. Children, it is now known, continue to wish that their parents remained married after they have split and even after their parents have each remarried and made new lives for themselves. It used to be thought that children would be better off if incompatible parents separated. It is now established, however, that children suffer such disruption and unhappiness during the divorce of their parents, and for years afterwards, that they are adversely affected in many different aspects of their lives.

Children whose parents have divorced may be affected socially, emotionally, in their educational achievements and financially; and, in their adult lives, in their ability to make successful relationships and in their career. It makes very good sense, therefore, to avoid divorce if at all possible, and to take every step to minimize the bad effects of divorce upon our children.

Are your children troubled?

Children are seldom capable of taking one or other parent aside and telling them that they feel guilty, angry, fearful or sad, although these are indeed the emotions most commonly experienced by children of separating parents. Children express their feelings much more effectively by what they do rather than by what they say.

Children may exhibit feelings of stress and conflict in any of the following ways:

- Clinging behaviour, unwillingness to leave you alone, whingeing and tendency to be weepy.

- Clumsiness and other possible manifestations of anxiety.

- Being unusually difficult or disobedient.

- Wanting to sleep in your bed.

- Aggressive behaviour, such as constant fighting with brother, sister and friends.

- Unwillingness to go to bed.

- Being withdrawn, difficult to engage emotionally.

- Tantrums and crying fits.

- Lying.

- Stealing.

- Bedwetting (at an age when this had long since ceased to be a problem).

- ▓ Unwillingness to leave you to go to school (perhaps feigning illness).

- ▓ Playing truant.

- ▓ Nightmares.

- ▓ Unexplained stomach ache, headache, nausea and other health problems.

- ▓ Depression (most people do not realize that children can become depressed, but the Department of Developmental Psychiatry at Cambridge University showed in 1991 that 14 per cent of all eleven- to sixteen-year-olds were exhibiting symptoms of depression).

It must be said that many of these signs are features of normal childhood and do not necessarily and exclusively indicate stress and conflict. Many of these signs may be exhibited by children at various stages of their development and may be part of their normal development. They may have their origins in other causes than in the separation of their parents, and they need to be seen in that perspective. The length of time the symptoms last, their severity, the effect they have on the child's life and whether or not they prevent the child from doing anything that might be regarded as customary should all be taken into account. For example, many children fight with their brothers and sisters and show themselves unwilling to go to bed. It is very much a matter of degree and intensity. Only you, as a parent, can know to what extent the child's behaviour has *changed*.

Parents are in a supreme position to alleviate their child's suffering. The child looks to her or his parent for total, unconditional support and love. The child believes in parents and in their ability to protect them from difficulties to a degree that will almost certainly not be rivalled by any other person for the rest of that child's life. However, parents may find it very difficult to help their own children, to acknowledge the cause of any emotional problems or to accept that behaviour has an emotional cause, and to communicate with their children in an uninvolved, detached and helpful way.

Parents can help in difficult emotional situations by offering their children support and love in an entirely unconditional way. In other words, rather than 'I won't love you any more if you're naughty,' it should be 'Come on, I love you and care about you – why are you being so naughty?' It is invariably better to coax, to persuade, to be gentle, rather than to criticize, to chastise or to reject. Take care not to push children if, for example, they are listless: 'Buck up, for goodness sake' is not likely to cut much ice. It is far better to try 'Come and do this with Mummy; I need your help and I like you being with me'.

By far the most significant cause of stress in children is the loss of a parent, either through bereavement or through the separation and divorce of the parents. It is still not sufficiently recognized how psychologically disturbing and destructive this is for children. They cannot fully understand the reasons for their parents' divorce and may even assume some of the blame for the event. It is at this time, and for several years afterwards, that children may need the most support.

One girl, whose parents' relationship eventually failed, says:

'I can hardly remember my Dad living at home. He used to come and go a lot. Mum said that he was working and sleeping at the hospital so that he could look after his patients. I still don't understand why he couldn't come and be with us.'

The value to children of minimizing the effects and inevitable outcome of a failing relationship or marriage cannot be over-emphasized, in both the short and the long term.

The reasons for divorce

The current legal grounds for divorce include adultery, unreasonable behaviour and separation on the basis of irreconcilable differences. These grounds conceal a multitude of difficulties within marriage, some of which could be resolved before divorce becomes inevitable, provided that both partners are prepared to negotiate and compromise.

What can go wrong within a marriage? Any of the following problems or situations can have adverse consequences for one or both partners:

- Sexual difficulties (usually a sign of other problems).

- Incessant and violent arguments about sex, money, children and household tasks.

- Profound changes in your life (having a baby, changing jobs or moving home, for example).

- Unfounded jealousy.

- Infidelity.

- Problems with a child or children.

- Falling out of love, growing apart and wanting different things from the marriage and from life.

- Alcohol or drug abuse.

When you become enmeshed in marital difficulties, it grows increasingly difficult to recall the positive aspects of the person to whom you are married and, indeed, why you married them at all. When the relationship becomes as fraught at this, it may take the intervention of a skilled professional marital counsellor to bring out the positive elements of a marriage and to help resolve the negative aspects.

'I look at her and I just wonder where the magic has gone,' grumbles a husband of his wife of nine years. 'She used to be fun, but now all she ever is is miserable. She looks a fright, she's put on a lot of weight, she never wants to do anything except watch the box. Sometimes I look at her as if she were a stranger. How could I ever have married her? What has she turned into? Even the children are affected by her moods. I just don't know what to do. It's a living hell.'

Can the marriage stand infidelity?

Here is one woman's reaction to her husband's infidelity:

> 'I went on holiday to Portugal one year with my husband, my best
> friend and her husband. I went for a walk one after noon and practically
> fell over my so-called best friend and my husband at it behind some
> rocks. That was the end. I never considered reconciliation. I threw him
> out of the house when we got back from holiday and sued for divorce
> straight away. I knew that I could never live with that sense of betrayal.
> What on earth did he think marriage was for?'

All the actions and events in our lives help to shape us and
make us what we are. Unless both partners are entirely detached
within their marriage (in which case it could be argued that it is
not in essence a marriage at all), an affair must have an impact.
Neither partner will regard the other in quite the same light as
before.

An affair, almost by definition, implies a degree of betrayal, deceit
and coldbloodedness on the part of the partner who has started the
affair. The spouse is unlikely to view her/his partner in quite the
same loving, unconditional way that she/he had until the matter of
the affair became known. The partner who has been unfaithful may,
in turn, suffer feelings of guilt, anger and remorse.

Most of us understand marriage as an exclusive contract, an
igloo, so to speak, to which there is only one entrance. Once this
exclusivity has been breached and the igloo is seen to have more
than one entrance, the innocent partner may become wary and
resentful. This atmosphere is not conducive to a happy and
harmonious marriage. The unspoken question 'Will she/he do it
again?' brings with it a sense of unease to the marital relationship.

All this is not to say that a marriage is irretrievably damaged by
an affair. Many people are enjoying marriages in which one of them
has had an affair in the past. While the marriage will not be the same
as it was before, it can mature and survive. The children, as well as
both partners, can benefit if both husband and wife accept
professional counselling in such a situation to help forgive and come
to terms with what has happened and to progress. Divorce is by no

means inevitable in such circumstances, but it takes time to come to terms with anger and a profound sense of betrayal, and with guilt. (Professional counselling can be obtained through your doctor, or, if you prefer, through Relate; details are given at the end of the book in Useful addresses.)

Infidelity is just one example of the possible causes of a broken marriage. Like all major problems within a marriage, it can be overcome provided that both parties are willing to try to do so. Very few problems are entirely and hopelessly insoluble.

Many people who contemplate divorce view it as a solution to their problems. It is not commonly recognized that divorce brings with it an entirely new set of problems. Many people are emotionally and financially worse off after divorce than before, particularly if they have children. The children, if they are to be entirely honest, may admit that they continue to regret the fact of their parents' divorce for many years afterwards. Such bereavement, for this is what divorce is for children, usually disturbs them acutely for some two years. It may take five years or more for full acceptance to be achieved.

'I used to hear them shouting at each other and talking about divorce,' says a young girl of twelve. 'It made me feel sick. I used to bury my head under the pillow and try to go to sleep. It's just Mum and me now so it's much quieter, but I still wish Dad lived here properly with us like he used to.'

Is the marriage or the relationship so bad that the only choice is to dissolve it?

RECOGNIZING DEPRESSION

You may be depressed if you are experiencing some or all of the following:

- **Profound and prolonged change of mood – do you feel depressed or are your friends and family remarking that you seem depressed?**

▩ An overwhelming sense of failure and self-blame.

▩ Suicidal thoughts and feelings.

▩ Loss of zest for life, affecting everything you do.

▩ Constant fatigue.

▩ Loss of appetite.

▩ Poor sleep and waking early in the morning.

▩ Cessation of menstrual periods.

▩ Generalized, unexplained anxiety.

▩ A feeling, above all, that you are not 'yourself'.

If you consider yourself depressed, consult your doctor without delay. She/he may offer you counselling, drug therapy or a specialist referral to a psychiatrist, who may offer a combination of psychotherapy and drug therapy. Do not forget that children, as well as adults, can become depressed.

2 Out in the open

*'We hadn't been getting on and I suppose we were completely wrapped
up in our own problems. My daughter's school report came in and I
was shattered to see just how badly she had been doing. She used to be
average or better in all subjects, but here I was, reading comments like
"poor concentration", "shows no interest in subject", "unreliable about
turning in written work on time". I just couldn't believe it. Anyway,
my husband looked at it and then rounded on me, saying that I was
too soft and was unfit to be a mother. The absolute blind injustice of
what he was saying really got to me. He knew perfectly well that before
our own troubles she was doing very well. There just hadn't been
anything to worry about before, as far as she was concerned. I realized
then that we would have to sort ourselves out one way or another.'*

Some research suggests that much of the damage inflicted upon
children of divorcing parents occurs in the period *before* the decision
to split up is taken and *before* the children have been told that their
parents are proposing to divorce.

Divorce is often regarded as a single life event, whereas in fact it
is a long-drawn-out process, a complex chain of events that
reverberates for many years. It is vital at each step that you regard it
as a *positive* process rather than a decision forced upon you. Being
positive, of course, depends on how much control you have over
the situation. You must remember that how much and how well
you can help your children adjust to your separation depends on
how well you yourself adjust.

It may be some time before parents are sufficiently certain that
they are going to separate and, therefore, some time before they tell
their children. (How best to do this is discussed in the next chapter.)

It is now, however, that the fabric of family life starts to wear thin. Parents are likely to be tired, stressed, depressed, angry and guilty. As a result, each may put more pressure than usual upon the other. Whereas either parent would once have been happy to take their son to cubs, for example, now neither has the energy and each wants the other to do it. What inference can their son draw from this other than that neither wants to be with him? Conversely, one or both parents may become *more* closely involved with the child and, perhaps, more possessive. As the pressure mounts, and pleasurable family activities take a back seat, the child senses that family life is not as it was.

> 'It was worse for us – my brother and my sisters – before they decided to split up,' remembers one daughter of parents who are now divorced. 'The not knowing was awful. At least once it was out in the open we knew where we were.'

Many children faced with this type of situation decline to ask questions at all. They fear the worst, feel that the deterioration of family life is somehow their fault, worry that no one is going to stay at home and look after them and start to feel that their parents are no longer a fixed point in their lives. The more they feel this, the more likely they are either to withdraw further into themselves or, on the other hand, to become increasingly clingy and weepy in apparently inappropriate situations. In this way even a trip to the supermarket, for example, can become an ordeal for the over-stressed parent.

The children who do ask questions are unlikely to fare better than those who do not, given that some questions are unanswerable and, in the case of those that can be answered, parents are often understandably reluctant to talk about something that is painful and that they are powerless to prevent or alter. Questions can be very wide-ranging:

▓ **Is Dad going to leave us?**

▓ **Will I still have to go to school if Dad leaves?**

▓ **What will happen to the kitten?**

- Why can't you love each other like a proper Mummy and Daddy?

- Is it because I dropped the milk bottle?

- Why is Mummy crying?

- Why does Mummy want to go to the doctor on her own? She usually takes me with her.

- Why is Daddy always working? He never comes and says goodnight to me any more.

- Why was Daddy sleeping on the sofa?

- Why isn't Daddy helping us with the shopping today?

- Why are you so cross with Mum?

No one would expect to go through a serious physical illness without advice, support and professional help. There is no reason, therefore, why anyone should expect to undergo a serious emotional experience without comparable support. Many people are instinctively wary of professional counselling services, for they view the acceptance of this kind of help as a sign of failure and weakness. Curiously, they do not view the support offered by friends as having the same sort of stigma. And yet the help and support offered by friends is similar to what is known as supportive psychotherapy.

This woman feels that she could have given counselling a try:

'We were going through quite a bad patch and I was getting pretty upset and I couldn't sleep. My doctor suggested that I have counselling – I knew that my husband would never agree to go – but it was just before Christmas and I was very busy. Things settled down over Christmas and the crisis seemed to be over. I had the opportunity of having counselling in January, but I told the doctor that I didn't think we needed it now. My husband left me in July after two months of behaving very peculiarly (for him). I realize now that had I had counselling in January, when things were calm, I could have benefited very greatly. Maybe we wouldn't have split up at all – and put his children through a second separation and divorce – or maybe it would just have helped me cope with what was to come. I should have gone. But, of course, one always hopes for the best. I thought that counselling would drag it all up again, but in fact it had never gone away – it was just simmering below the surface.'

What is marriage guidance?

Marriage guidance offers facilities for couples to discuss, negotiate and compromise over their problems in a full and totally frank manner. The presence of a trained counsellor enables sensible, logical discussion and means that fullblown arguments, usually ruinous to discussion, are analysed in the hope of extracting some truth that is meaningful to both parties. Even in the event of one partner failing to co-operate fully, both, with the help of a professional counsellor, will usually come away from sessions having learned something.

Marriage guidance is about uncovering hidden problems, bringing issues out into the open and discussing them in the hope of resolving them. Marriage guidance is not about saving marriages at all costs. It is about enabling the two partners to communicate successfully. This does not mean that they communicate, necessarily, in order to prolong the marriage. If one partner has decided to end it, marriage guidance can enable as mature a separation and divorce as is possible, if the couple goes through with that decision, as this divorced mother's experience illustrates:

'The counsellor made us see how we were using the children in our differences with each other and how we made the children feel anxious and fearful. Professional support didn't stop us breaking up – that was inevitable – but it showed us how to recognize our anger and channel it rather than making things even worse for the children than they already were.'

Marriage guidance can also refer the couple to local mediation services which will assist both partners to organize and negotiate their separation without bitterness.

Where to get marriage guidance

Ask your doctor to refer you to a trained marital therapist or marriage guidance counsellor on the National Health Service. Alternatively, consult Relate or London Marriage Guidance Council, both of which charge (details of both are given at the end of the book in Useful addresses).

If you decide upon a private therapist of your own choice, be sure to check a word-of-mouth recommendation with a professional opinion. Anyone can set themselves up as a private marriage guidance counsellor.

What happens?

There is a tremendous variation in the nature and direction of discussion, as it depends on the two partners, the problems and the counsellor's method, expertise and empathy.

Whom can it help?

Marriage guidance can help anyone who genuinely wants to be helped, provided that the therapist is sufficiently skilled and experienced. Counsellors are less likely to be able to help someone who is attending only reluctantly, but many become less reluctant after experiencing counselling themselves. Men are often not keen to consult a counsellor, but that does not mean that women cannot derive benefit by attending alone.

'My girlfriend wanted me to come to counselling with her for the sake of our children if nothing else. But, honestly, it just looked like the ultimate exercise in masochism to me,' was one young father's opinion. Another, however, was very positive: 'I was very surprised by how skilful the mediators were. At first I thought that at least one of them, if not both, were on my wife's side, but I realized that was just one of their strategies. Really, they were brilliant.'

What if you don't like the counsellor?

If you or your partner can see the potential of counselling but happen not to like or feel in tune with the counsellor, do not hold back about finding another. If the one you are seeing was recommended by your doctor, do not hesitate to explain the problem and ask whether she/he can refer you to someone else. Don't be afraid to change if you experience this common problem.

The advantages of seeing a professional counsellor include the facts that they are properly trained, they know how to retain a professional detachment (when they would otherwise become emotionally involved themselves) and the client can walk away after a session without having to offer the therapist some similar sort of emotional support. In other words, the client can unload and, at the same time, benefit from professional advice without being indebted in any way.

Counselling is, by its nature, non-judgemental. This means that you are entirely free to say what you like and admit things you may have done without fear of invoking any sense of shock or horror from the therapist. You will be invited to explore how you feel about what you may have said or done, but you will not be judged in any sense. Equally, you may discuss with your therapist things your partner may have said or done. Again, because of the non-judgemental nature of counselling, your therapist will not express any sympathy, or disgust, or any other personal reaction. She/he will simply enable *you* to clarify *your* feelings – as this man's experience bears out:

'I thought the counsellor would give us advice, but she didn't. Yet somehow she enabled us to work things out for ourselves without really seeming to say much herself. I don't think we would have managed as well without her.'

As stated earlier, divorce is not so much an event as a long-drawn-out process. It is often preceded by trial separation under the guise of 'I need a bit of a break' or 'We just need some space'. Trial separations do not invariably result in divorce, but divorce is characteristically preceded by one or both partners trying to break away and then returning. If you have any desire at all for the marriage not only to survive but also to flourish, this is the time to take stock, to reassess and, if you wish, to go for counselling either singly or together.

Some people believe that counselling only one partner cannot be effective in bringing change. Experts in marital therapy, however, are divided on this. Some believe that counselling can work only if both partners are involved, others disagree. My own belief is that one partner will benefit to some extent when the other person does not participate, but that the benefit will be greater if both attend.

Serious problems need to be discussed and resolved. Trying to overlook them does not work for long: they usually resurface. Effective negotiation and compromise, however, can either benefit the marriage or, at the least, can minimize the damage to both partners and to their children.

TYPES OF THERAPIST

Psychiatrist: Is a medically qualified doctor with additional higher qualification in psychiatry. Can prescribe drugs – for example, for depression.

Psychologist: Has a degree in psychology and a diploma in clinical psychology. Not a doctor and cannot therefore prescribe drugs.

Counsellor: Has taken a basic training course in counselling. Some so-called counsellors have no training at all, but can nevertheless be effective.

Disruption and discord

It used to be thought that so-called broken homes were responsible, in themselves, for children's problems. Some research shows that it may be the disruption and discord preceding divorce that does the damage. Children may suffer all sorts of problems either at the time or later in life. The Exeter Family Study (1994), carried out in the UK by Monica Cockett and Dr John Tripp, showed for the first time just how much separation undermines children's sense of self-worth and their physical and mental health generally.

Research in the UK and elsewhere has clearly shown that children are often miserable and insecure when they have to listen to frequent parental arguments. Although parents try not to quarrel in front of their children, most children are aware of their parents' differences. In the Exeter Family Study most children said that they had not expected their parents' problems to lead to separation, even though they were unhappy about their parents' rows. Children in violent, abusive marriages were glad when the marriages ended; but, for many, even when they were aware of parental conflict, the loss of one parent from the home had come as a shock. Those children who were not exposed to parental quarrels, or silences and moods, or where there were no quarrels found their parents' separation even more perplexing.

The ways in which parental quarrels upset children are not always easy to understand. It seemed clear in the Exeter Family Study that from the children's point of view certain levels and kinds of disagreements were more upsetting than others.

In the families where parental conflict had resulted in divorce, the children did not always accept that divorce was the only solution. Conflict is also a feature of many intact family lives, and while this is known to have adverse effects on children, the study showed that loss of a parent was equally important.

Other research also suggests that children's behaviour and educational achievement is affected by parental conflict long before it comes to divorce. Children who have been exposed to violence between their parents are even more likely to be traumatized.

Some research shows that violent rows between parents who are deeply at odds with one another can cause more damage to the children than the actual family breakup, with one parent moving out of the family home.

Parents for life

It is vitally important for parents to remember that this is a role they have for life. A parental relationship is not one that they can relinquish when it is no longer personally happy and fulfilling. Although parents may decide, after serious consideration, that the marriage can no longer work, they may need to be helped to understand that the parental relationship should continue for life.

Renate Olins, director of the London Marriage Guidance Council, expresses it succinctly: 'Anything that lessens the bitterness will reduce the long-term damage and is greatly to the benefit of the next generation.'

Very few people can claim to have managed a pleasantly civilized divorce. Nearly every couple is guilty of tit-for-tat behaviour, open rows, trying to get the children on their side and running down their spouse.

One child featured in the *Panorama* television programme, 'For the Sake of the Children' (screened in the UK in February 1994), was reported to have collapsed at just two and a half. Her mother explained: 'She had a total nervous breakdown. I didn't see it coming because you don't think of children having nervous breakdowns. She became incontinent, she didn't move, she was totally traumatized.'

Thelma Fisher, director of the National Association of Family Mediation and Conciliation Services, said at the end of 1995: 'It is startling how many people who have been unable to speak to one another, let alone hear what the other has to say, will end up wanting to work things out. Most parent want to do what's best for their children and they come to see that mediation might help them do that rather than using them to punish the other partner.'

Healthy routines

At no time is it more important to try to keep to domestic routines in order to minimize the sense of disruption and looming chaos that characterizes the period before separation. An effort of will needs to be made, for the sake of the children, to keep up the usual shopping, cooking, cleaning and washing routines of family life. This at least gives the children some sense of normality around them. Make sure that they continue to do their homework, to see their friends, to care for their pets and so on. These routines are invaluable not only for your children but for you, too.

As well as these practical routines, it is important also to try to maintain a positive and reasonably cheerful outlook – again, by helping your children you will be helping yourself. Everything may seem black, but if you allow yourself to start thinking this way, it will seem worse and you will also start to alienate friends and the people who could help you. A pessimistic, negative view of life can influence our life events, the things that happen to us and our reactions to those events. 'Life is what you make it' has become a cliché because it's true.

If you think positively, and make active attempts not to dwell on negative events more than you have to, you are more likely to do well at work, to have happy relationships with those around you and to feel good about yourself. Optimists tend to fare better and experience fewer disappointments, partly because of their sunnier outlook on life, which is in itself attractive to others.

Looking after yourself

It is even more important, during difficult times, to try to remember to look after yourself. Do you manage to have some time to yourself every week? If not, can you arrange for this by having a friend look after your children for a few hours each week? Having time to think and just to be alone are important elements of your emotional wellbeing. There should, ideally, be some balance between the three main areas of your life:

- Your work self: this includes paid work, housework, community work and any unpaid work.

- Your relationship self: this includes your immediate family, your friends, your extended family and your colleagues.

- Your individual self: this includes your physical wellbeing, your intellectual activities, your emotional and spiritual health.

Do you feel that you have the correct balance between your three selves? Each one interreacts with the other. Positive energy generated in one aspect nourishes the others. Equally, a crisis in your personal life, for example, will affect your work self and your individual self. Make sure, then, that you have some quiet time for yourself and that your life is not entirely made over to the service of others. Don't try to do everything yourself. Try to set priorities and delegate tasks whenever you can. Don't, for the moment, do those things that aren't absolutely essential: use the time for yourself instead. By refreshing yourself in this way you will be better able to look after your children and to withstand the stresses of a deteriorating marriage. Mundane it may sound, but at no time is it more important to eat regularly and well, to cut down on drinking and smoking, to reduce caffeine, to get some fresh air and exercise every day and to go to bed at roughly the same time each night. Don't allow yourself to become involved in rows late at night: nothing could make you less likely to get a good night's sleep. Just walk away from it.

It is when separation or divorce becomes inevitable that you will need to draw on your deepest reserves. Telling the children, the subject of the next chapter, is one of the ordeals that separating parents have to face.

3 Telling the children

'My Mum took us to our Gran's — for a holiday, she said it was. We thought we'd be staying for a week or so, but then Mum said that we were going to stay on. I kept thinking that we would go home soon and we would see Dad but we never did. She never explained to us what was going on.'

Once the decision is made to break up the family, sooner or later the children need to be told what is happening and how it will affect them. This should be done as early as practicable.

Accepting the prevailing circumstances and the realization that the fruitless bickering, rows and silences might lead to a permanent separation is the hardest part of all — for children and for parents.

Many people in the throes of separation and eventual divorce are so upset, disturbed and confused themselves that they are unable to cope properly with discussing the matter with their children.

This is a time of great turbulence, change in a number of aspects of everyday life and, to a greater or lesser extent, chaos. At no time, therefore, is it more important that the children involved are given adequate explanations and full and convincing reassurances about their own future.

All of us flourish within a reasonably stable environment, but in the case of young children this is especially important. Very young children are not fully able to cope with inconsistency of care, material or emotional insecurity, or with sweeping changes in their lives. It is because separation and divorce bring so many different changes — typically a different place to live, a different family, less money — that children suffer.

Children are generally not very likely to ask a lot of questions when they truly fear the worst. Although they may have observed all the signs of a failing marriage, they will assume that this is normal and they do not anticipate that a difficult marriage will be brought to an end, thus causing them to lose either their mother or, more likely, their father. Even when one parent has left the family home, the children may still desist from putting questions. This is particularly likely to be the case if they realize that the resident parent is extremely upset by the separation. Once children are aware that questions prompt deeper sadness and more tears, they learn not to ask, despite the fact that not knowing may amount to a torment for them.

'My father never spoke to me about my mother once she had left,' said one child. 'He never gave us a reason for why she had left. She was living close by and sometimes we saw her. When we were older, we were able to go and see her, but when we were still very young we had no contact. I used to cry myself to sleep every night. There wasn't anyone I could ask about it, or talk to about it. It's not the sort of thing you talk about. My Dad was very sad, which made me feel frightened. I didn't want to make him feel worse.'

When to tell the children?

It is very difficult to know when you should tell your children of an impending separation. Indeed, this may not always be possible; in many cases one partner simply walks out without having considered the children's reaction.

This was the experience of one nine-year-old: 'Dad had already left once, although I don't remember that first time. But the main time was on Christmas Day. It was just after lunch. I didn't understand why he left – I thought it must be something that I did. My mother was crying and sobbing. The woman next door came in and talked to her for a bit. I kept thinking he'd come back soon, but he didn't. I do see him now, but I never see him at Christmas.'

Clearly, the distress that will be caused to the children by the completely unexpected departure of one parent should be avoided. It should always be possible for adults, for the sake of the children involved, to try to wait at least one more week so that both parents can talk to the children and reassure them. In this way it will be possible to go some way to avoid inflicting a profound emotional shock upon them.

It would be better still if both parents were able to talk together to the child or children, preferably one child at a time, some weeks before the separation is to take place. If the matter is handled in this way, the departing parent can tell the children why he is leaving and where he will be living, and make arrangements for regular visits with the children. He can explain that he and the mother are no longer able to live happily together and that, although he is leaving her, he is not leaving the children. He can explain that he is and always will be their father and that this will not change. He can reassure the children that he loves them very much and that he will be looking forward to seeing them. He can also explain that he is better able to be the parent that the children deserve if he no longer lives with Mum.

If the child is at boarding school, he or she should be told *during* the school holidays, but not right at the end of the holidays. It is grossly unfair to tell the child when she or he is away at school, and this should be avoided if at all possible.

How much to tell them?

First and foremost, it is important to give your children an explanation that they can understand. Many children do not grasp what exactly is meant by the expression 'we are divorcing'. They know that divorce is serious, but nevertheless the word has little meaning for some children, particularly young ones. This leaves them vulnerable to picking up half-understood truths from the school playground, such as 'divorce means you get a new house and a new daddy'.

So tell them only when you are ready to give a full and meaningful explanation of what separation is going to mean for them. You should cover these points:

▧ **Which parent will continue to look after them, feed them, clothe them and so on.**

- Which parent will leave the family home.

- Where the resident parent and children will live – that is, whether they will stay in the same home or move to a new home.

- Where the non-resident parent will live.

- When the children will see the non-resident parent and how often.

- What will happen about holidays.

- Whether they will continue going to the same school, even if they have to move home.

- Whether it is all right for them to tell their friends – many children try to keep their parents' separation secret without realizing that so many other children are in the same position.

Then:

- Reassure them that they will still be able to see their friends – nothing will change in that way.

- Reassure them that their pets will be coming too, if moving home is envisaged.

'They don't want to know'

Many parents are deceived into believing that their children genuinely do not want to know about what's happening because the children show so little interest. They nod mutely at the information they are given and do not ask questions. This does not mean that they are not disturbed by the family atmosphere and the sense of impending change, simply that they are too frightened to want to face it.

How often to tell them

Many researchers have noted that even in cases where children have been given full and careful explanations, they later claim not to have been told very much or not to have been told at all. Again this can be attributed to fear, to panic or to misery: they do not want to hear what they are being told. (As another example of this phenomenon, it is well documented that when a patient has a consultation with a hospital specialist, the patient forgets a substantial part of what the doctor has said.) Because of this, it is important for your children's wellbeing, in both the short and the long term, to tell them at each and every appropriate moment that you love them, you will always be there to look after them and that the other parent will always continue to be their parent even if she/he no longer lives with you.

Where can the children get additional support?

'My husband left me for another woman,' said a twenty-nine-year-old mother, 'and I found it extremely hard to cope with two children under the age of five. I was in a terrible state myself. I remember my husband telling me to call an old friend of his who'd always been fond of me because, as he said, "I can't help you, I'm the one that caused it." That was all very well, but what about the children. Who were they meant to call?'

You will find that kindly people, sometimes even the most unexpected, will rally round at difficult times. The important thing is never to be afraid and never be too proud to ask for help. Both you and your children can benefit if you involve the people close to you.

- Tell your parents and your partner's parents what is happening so that they can offer practical and emotional support. If they offer to look after the children for an afternoon, be glad to accept. The children may find it easier to talk to one of them than to their mother or father.

- If you are on good terms with your neighbours, invite them in for a cup of coffee and let the children realize that they know and that they can be relied upon to be friendly and helpful.

■ If your children have godparents, who are after all chosen in order to offer moral and spiritual guidance, let them visit or take the children to visit them.

■ The children's own friends – their peer group – can offer invaluable support in quite different ways from the adults around them. If they ask to invite friends in, don't hesitate to agree, even though this may pose an additional strain for you. If they ask to stay at a friend's for a sleepover, again, agree without hesitation. Do everything you can to facilitate their friendships.

■ Close family friends can be a great help. Now is the time to see those friends who have known your children all their young lives and let them do whatever they can to minimize the pain that the children may be suffering. If you have friends who would be willing to take them to the cinema, or leisure centre, or skating rink – or something of the children's own choice – be happy to accept. People usually find it much easier to offer this kind of practical support rather than emotional support.

Your children's teachers

Many parents believe that they should tell their child's teachers once it is known that a separation is to take place. In many cases this is undoubtedly a well-founded belief, and the teacher may be warmer and more understanding to a difficult child, or, to phrase it more exactly, a child who is experiencing difficulties at home.

There are drawbacks, however, to the child's teacher being acquainted with the facts of parental separation. Some people still see divorce as a stigma, and the teacher may thus be on the lookout for the child to behave badly or turn in poor work. Some children are reported as feeling that if their teacher knows, it will be profoundly embarrassing and the teacher will show them pity in class. Most children hate to be singled out for special attention and this is what they fear will happen if you tell the school about family problems.

Research in the USA reveals that many teachers have not been able to show the children of divorcing parents the support the parents could have wished for and, therefore, in many cases no useful purpose has been served in telling them. Some research in Britain and in the USA shows that in cases in which teachers are aware of family reorganization they may expect the child to have difficulties. This may colour their attitude and their expectations of responses from the child.

The question of whether or not to tell your child's teachers is clearly a complex one and can be resolved only according to the individual merits of each particular case. You are the person in the best position to understand your child and to be able to predict what is best for her or him in the situation. Clearly, if you have relatively close contact with the school and you enjoy good relations with your child's teachers, it may be best to tell them.

At the least keep an eye on your child's homework, attend PTA meetings and study your child's reports so that you are fully aware of how your child is managing life outside the home.

Finally, although children often find it hard to speak to anyone about what is happening at home, most depend on each other for support and often talk to each other more than they do to their schoolteachers.

Children's feelings

The *Panorama* television programme 'For the Sake of the Children' interviewed one mother who had embarked on her third marriage and by now had five children. 'You think if you terminate that situation and create a new one . . . you assume that they'll all be better for it,' she said. 'When you're busy making a mess of your life, you actually want to look round and see that it's not affecting them. You make this bargain in your mind and you think, right, I'm being honest and I'm explaining what's happening and the whys, and this child is then appearing to cope and appearing to accept and lead a normal life. And, in actual fact, all it is is a front . . . it's just a protective barrier they put up.'

The children of separating parents are virtually without exception deeply shocked. Very few are glad to see the departure of one of their parents, no matter how openly awful the marriage may have been. Children, just like adults, run the full gamut of emotions on being told what is to happen. Unlike adults, they do not have the emotional maturity to be able to cope with such disturbing and distressing emotions. Unlike adults, again, they have no control of the situation: they have not sought a separation from their parents. Their emotions may run through any or all of the following at different times:

- **Denial, when they simply don't believe what they are being told.**

- **Shock.**

- **Anger.**

- **Conflict.**

- **Anxiety.**

- **Uncertainty.**

- **Loneliness.**

- **Guilt.**

- **Shame.**

- **Misery.**

When there are difficulties, children can suffer a crisis period which may last for as long as two years – and this is a very long time in a young child's life. It may take children five years or more to achieve a complete acceptance and understanding of the loss of one of their parents. The grief caused by divorce, which is the subject of Chapter 4, is normally experienced in four stages, which typically overlap one another: denial, anger, sadness, acceptance. Girls are less likely to show their anger, while boys are more likely to become aggressive, sometimes at school rather than in the home.

Children's feelings are typically expressed by an increasingly chaotic lifestyle, paying less attention to school work and homework, being late to bed and late to school, and by developing psychosomatic illnesses, which keep them away from school. It should be remembered that these illnesses (typically, headache, stomach ache and nausea) are no less real to children for the fact that they have been caused by their emotional circumstances rather than by physical illness. Equally, as a parent, you should always bear in mind that children can become genuinely ill as well as reacting to the separation of their parents. Beware, then, of attributing all symptoms exclusively to your children's state of mind. Do not hesitate to seek the advice of your family doctor whenever you are in any doubt about your children's health. Children may have a problem in one of several areas of their live rather than in all areas.

Taking care of yourself

Your ability to help your children adjust to their new situation depends very largely on your own ability to come to terms with the situation yourself and to look after yourself sensibly so that you do not become totally exhausted and emotionally drained. Although looking after your children and your work must be priorities, remind yourself from time to time that, above all else, eating and sleeping are the two most essential priorities for survival.

Separation and divorce are, by their nature, stressful, so take care to watch for the signs and symptoms of stress:

▨ **Significant disturbance of sleep, including not being able to get to sleep, not being able to enjoy uninterrupted sleep, waking up much earlier than usual in the morning, and falling asleep during the day.**

▨ **Change in appetite** – eating much less or much more.

▨ **Weight gain or loss.**

▧ Reduced zest for life. In general, people have an interest in life. We each have different thresholds of zest. Few of us feel very zesty in the early morning. Stress is indicated by a marked loss of interest in life.

▧ Irritability.

▧ Confusion.

▧ Forgetfulness to a greater degree than usual.

▧ Feeling anxious or panicky.

All of these signs are significant and should not be ignored if they persist for more than two to three weeks. You will probably benefit from talking to your family doctor and perhaps a professional counsellor as well (your doctor can refer you to one). Marriage guidance and counselling is discussed in Chapter 2.

Taking care of yourself means attending to your individual needs, in order best to care for your children. Look at the following ten suggestions and see what you can do to help yourself. You owe it to yourself and to your children to take control of your life in any way that is available to you:

1   Get in touch with one or two of your close friends and have a long chat.

2   Make a habit of going for a brisk, long walk, several times a week if possible.

3   Decide on some type of exercise (aerobics, swimming, squash, tennis, riding, running, for example) and get into the habit of going twice a week.

4   Review what you eat. Cut out sugary and salty foods. Cut down on protein and increase your carbohydrate and fibre intake. Explore different gourmet ways of cooking vegetables and pasta with unusual herbs and spices.

5   Treat yourself in any way you wish – perhaps by buying something new to wear, arranging a cinema or theatre outing or going out for a delicious meal.

6   Think of someone who would appreciate your help and company and do something for them. You may be surprised at how much this benefits *you*.

7   Try one or two of the alternative health therapies – massage, perhaps, or acupuncture. Explain to the therapist that you are feeling stressed.

8   Write down your long-term priorities and goals and think hard about the ways in which you can achieve them.

9   Is there a skill you have always wanted to acquire? This is the time to consider taking lessons or teaching yourself.

10   As a cathartic exercise, have a good bout of cleaning, gardening or sorting out cupboards and throwing away what you never use.

YOUR CHILD IS NOT ALONE

Once your child realizes that some of her or his classmates are in the same position, she or he may be able to derive considerable support from friends. However, many children try to keep the knowledge of their parents' failing marriage a secret, perhaps out of a sense of guilt or shame. Bear the following figures in mind so that you can explain to your child, with conviction, that many other families undergo the sort of changes she or he is experiencing:

- In Sweden, Denmark and the UK two out of five marriages end in divorce.

- In the USA and Russia only one in two marriages survive.

- In southern European countries one in ten marriages flounders.

- As divorce rates increase, marriages break up sooner and therefore the children of divorced parents are, year by year, progressively younger.

- In the USA one in two children is likely to experience the breakup of their parents' marriage – the highest rate in the world.

- One in four children in England and Wales experiences the divorce of their parents.

Explain to your child gently that, although this is very upsetting and hurtful for us, it does happen to other families as well. We are not the only ones.

Torn in two

In conclusion, children have great difficulty in accepting that they can love both parents when neither of them loves each other: 'If Mum doesn't want him here, he must be bad.' Young children have boundless faith in their parents' judgements, and it therefore often sets up unbearable conflicts for them when their parents are seen openly not only to disagree but to find it impossible to live with each other. When children are told that, on the one hand, their parent is about to leave them and, on the other, that that same parent loves them just the same, again, unbearable conflicts may be created. The situation of separation and divorce demands of children an emotional maturity that most are simply too young to possess. The more you, as their parent, can do to help them through a difficult, and potentially damaging, period in their lives, the better they will be able to cope in both the short and the long term.

4 Losing a parent

'It just hurts when they talk about it and I don't think I'm ready yet to know what went on really. I look around me and most of my friends have got parents together and they didn't have problems like I did when I was younger. So, in some ways, that's why it hurts so much.'

Dr Sebastian Kraemer, a consultant child and adolescent psychiatrist at the Tavistock Centre in London, explains: 'The whole thing is very easily covered up. Provided he or she can get to school, provided they have some kind of semblance of a normal life, everybody is very keen to keep wraps on the whole thing. That is, I think, quite a common experience, so the hidden pain is really unbearable. Children don't want to ask about the divorce, parents don't want to talk about it, and that's one very powerful reason for the conspiracy of silence about the painful effects of divorce.' (Both Dr Kraemer and the girl quoted above were interviewed on the *Panorama* television programme, 'For the Sake of the Children', February 1994.)

Consultant paediatrician Dr John Tripp comments: 'We know that conflict is damaging in the sense that it undermines children's wellbeing and makes them feel less good about themselves when their parents fight, but our data suggest that this is only part of the reason for the effects that we see when a parents leaves the home.'

Other specialists working in the field agree that it may not be the conflict before separation and divorce that damages children the most. Recent work on the National Child Development Study (1958) also casts doubt on the fact that conflict before divorce is the most significant factor in causing long-term problems for children. Monica Cockett and Dr Tripp found, during the course of their research for the Exeter Family Study that, although children knew that their parents argued, they had not expected them to part.

Why did he have to go?

The following case history, which is featured in full in Catherine Itzin's fascinating book *Splitting Up: Single Parent Liberation*, illustrates just how much children are prepared to put up with in their need for two parents:

'At this stage the children were completely non-existent to him. Absolutely. He used to go away. It was a regular thing every weekend. And I would say to him, "Well, I don't give a damn any more where you're going but just leave a phone number in case I need you in an emergency." And one weekend I did. Sarah was rushed into hospital. There I was with all the kids and I didn't know what to do. He rolled home about eleven that Sunday night, and I said, "Where have you been? Sarah's been taken to hospital and I needed you." He just went round to the hospital to see if she was okay, and that was it. He was really irresponsible about the kids. He would promise to play football with them or take them to a match, and when it came to the day he would just ignore them and say he had things of his own to do. Steven's face would just crumple. And there was nothing I could say or do. I would just say something insignificant to them – like never mind. What can you do? I couldn't do a lot of things with Steven that Alf should have been doing. I had babies.

'There were rows every day. And the children must have been aware of it all. They were very heavy fights. I would wait up all night for him, and I would say to myself, "I'm not going to say anything to him. I'm going to let him see that I don't care." But by the time he came in at two or three in the morning I'd be worked up into a state, so that it was impossible not to say anything. He would make the most ridiculous excuses for not coming home. They were classic, really classic. In the end he would have *me* apologizing to *him* for rowing and for questioning him! How dare I question him! You disgusting person for losing your temper! I'm much too superior to lose my temper. Look at you, you hysterical, horrible woman! He would laugh. He wouldn't even have a proper row with me. He would laugh at me. He would goad me something terrible. I would get madder and I did sometimes pick up a knife to him with the wish to kill him. I really felt murder for him, because he couldn't even have the decency to have a dignified row with me. He would accuse *me* of having affairs! I put that down to his guilty conscience. And I would end up trying to convince him that I wasn't having these affairs – these imaginary affairs! . . .

'I knew he was eventually going to leave. In fact it turned out *I* finally said, "Get the hell out of it."

'It was just before Christmas, four years ago this Christmas. He was gradually taking his clothes out. It wasn't just one fell swoop, of packing and going. He was gradually easing his way out. And it was Christmas Eve. He came and spent Christmas Eve with us and then he went. We'd been invited to a Christmas party and I was all prepared to go by myself, but he appeared and came with me. We didn't speak the whole evening and he brought me home, dropped me at the flat and went off. And then he actually went. He took all his things and went. Then about three weeks later there was a knock on the door one Sunday night – I'd just put the kids to bed – and he knocked at the door and he said, "I'm back. Here I am. Let's carry on."

'And I just said, "No! This really is the finish. I don't want you here any more." Unfortunately, my children heard all this. Heard me telling him to go. And *that* made things very difficult. Alf was so flabbergasted, because all our life together I'd given in to him completely, taking him back when he wanted to come, having sex when he wanted to. He was just so flayed that I could have refused him. I think he walked out more in anger that I refused him, because he had such a high opinion of himself, than because I didn't actually want *him*, if you can see what I mean.

'Anyway, I had terrible trouble. David was hysterical, absolutely hysterical. He was six. I went to Steven and explained to him. And he said, "You don't have to say anything. I understand more than you give me credit for." But the other one, David . . . to him I was the witch, the villain. And I had a terrible time with him for about a year. He started wetting the bed. And he wouldn't let me come near him. Even now if I go to touch him, he pushes me aside. You can't get close to him. All men were absolutely taboo. At that time, he had a male teacher, and he wouldn't go to school. I was pushing him in the morning and they were pulling him the other end. And he cried all day at school. He used to say he had stomach ache – which was just tension. This went on for about a year. He was petrified of his teacher. He rejected me and he was frightened of men. He was very confused. I think five to six is an incredibly vulnerable age, because they know everything and they can't understand anything. Steven was at the age when he knew and understood, at the age of nine. Sarah was too young, really, to know anything. But David . . . well, he thought all the years of our life together, though very bad . . . well . . . that's all he knew. That's what he thought everyone's life was like, and I'd ruined it for him as far as he was concerned.

'Then when it came to the crunch, when Alf was actually going, when we separated and there wasn't going to be anybody there . . . well, I was the villain of the piece. I had made the situation. And I had ruined his world completely. David couldn't look on it that I did it because I was in an impossible situation, that I was doing it for his good. Because the rows and slanging matches that they had to listen to were just terrible, horrific.

'. . . I didn't like him any more – his character, his attitude towards the children most of all. Whatever he felt towards me shouldn't have made any difference to the kids.'

Worse than death

Divorce is known, according to stress league tables, to be second only to bereavement in terms of its effect on individuals. While this may well be true for adults, the divorce of their parents is worse for children, emphatically so, than the death of one of their parents. The conflicts and anxieties created by the loss of a parent through divorce are practically unbearable for a child. Research going back some twenty years confirms that divorce is, indeed, worse for children than bereavement.

When a parent dies, the child is not very likely to hear all sorts of awful things being related about what that parent did in her/his lifetime. It is more likely that the deceased parent will be remembered with a fond sadness, affection and humour. In separation and divorce the resident parent may be feeling very angry at the breakdown of the marriage and with her/his former partner. It is extremely difficult in these circumstances to present the child with the sort of idealized picture that a bereaved child is offered. In death, time slowly heals the child's loss; but in divorce the child is more often than not given the opportunity of seeing the absent parent, which can have the effect of emphasizing the fact that the parent has left the child. The wound is repeatedly reopened.

Never in death does the child have to choose between the two parents, as this child, interviewed in the *Panorama* television programme has to: 'I find it difficult, like, because if I'm with my Dad, I miss my Mum a lot, if I'm with my Mum I miss my Dad. I just find it really difficult. I wish I could, like, live in the middle of them and I could visit my Mum the same and my Dad the same.'

In divorce, furthermore, the child may lose half of her relatives, while in death many of the relatives will offer valuable support.

The effects of losing a parent through divorce

By the early 1980s one-quarter of the children who had experienced the divorce of their parents were under five years of age. By the end of the decade that proportion had jumped to one-third. Some of these children live in perpetual fear for many, many months, sometimes years. The main effects are these:

■ They fear that they may never see the departing parent again.

■ They fear being abandoned.

■ They fear losing day-to-day contact.

■ They become less confident in their social relationships – they fear being left by someone they like or love.

■ Their confidence in their resident parent is undermined. They become disillusioned. They learn at a very early age that their emotional investment in a close relationship may not be worth it. They do not have the emotional maturity, however, fully to understand this, nor do they understand the reasons for their loss. 'If you stop loving him, you might stop loving us,' is their secret fear.

- They resent their parents' separation, as happened in the case of David above.

- Very many children continue to fantasize about the possibility of their parents' reunion years after the separation, sometimes even years after their parents' divorce. They genuinely believe that a reconciliation is possible and actively work on it, trying to bring their two parents together and avoiding doing anything that they perceive as making this event less likely to happen. They learn to bottle up their feelings and they make big efforts to be 'good' so that neither parent is inadvertently angered.

- Many children see a divorce as an option that their parents selected without taking the child's wishes into account: 'Why didn't they ask me what I thought?' And this makes the child feel powerless, which may create anger towards one or both parents, particularly the resident parent.

- They feel general confusion, which undermines their self-confidence and self-esteem. 'They never told me why,' is a frequently voiced cry from the heart. Because their understanding of the situation is limited and they can't make sense of 'Daddy's leaving, but he still loves you', they fear that Mum may go too, in the same inexplicable way, leaving them on their own.

The degrees of worry experienced by a child on the loss of a parent may vary, of course, with the age of the particular child. Many small children, for example, worry about who will take care of them. Similarly, anxiety can result in a preoccupation with the fear that their basic needs, such as food, will be overlooked.

Many children of nine to ten years old, so some research shows, felt their father to be entirely unavailable to them once their parents had separated: 'When Dad first left, I used to ring him every day. I was five then. He hardly ever rang me. I didn't ring him so often as I became older. I remember one terrible time, though, I got his answerphone – the message was said by his new wife. I didn't really understand it and I got very upset. I think I was about nine. Then my Mum got very angry that there was only an answerphone for me to talk to, so she rang it and left a message. And then Dad rang and she got angry again. In the end I didn't want to speak to him.'

Being left out in the cold

American researchers Judith S. Wallerstein and Joan B. Kelly observe in their impressive book *Surviving the Breakup: How Children and Parents Cope with Divorce:* 'It is likely that the ease with which older children were coopted as allies in the marital battles was related to their fears of being left out in the cold unless they joined the battles and demonstrated their continuing usefulness to the parent.'

Fear of abandonment is a central theme in the worries of most children who have been, as they see it, deserted by one of their parents. Many of them will do anything within their power to prevent a second desertion by the remaining parent. Others become, by contrast, aggressive, unruly, volatile, bossy or arrogant as part of a complex system of defences, which they feel they need to develop just to survive on a day-to-day basis, in order not to cry and feel sad and profoundly lonely.

One of the dreadful effects of marital separation, for children, is when their worst fears appear to be realized. It is the case in many families, before the separation, that the mother stayed at home and looked after the children. She would be there to greet them when they returned home and give them tea. A typical post-separation or post-divorce picture is of the children returning home alone to an empty, cold house. The resident parent is less able to do things for the children, because she is more tired and more stressed than she used to be and she also, typically, has less money to spend on games and outings. Not only is she now almost solely responsible for looking after the children and the home, but she is also herself adjusting to a new lifestyle. On top of all this, she is probably having to find additional time in which to manage the various stages in the legal process of divorce with her solicitor. Little wonder, then, that many children of separated parents feel that they are less important to their parents, less central to their lives. And, in consequence, their general sense of self-esteem diminishes accordingly. This in itself creates problems within the children's friendships: as they become less and less secure, they become increasingly prickly and moody and, in turn, not only are they less likely to be able to continue existing friendships in a satisfying way but also less likely to make new friends.

Another illustration of children's fear that they may be left out in the cold – and this is experienced by the majority of children – is that they yearn for their absent parent, but, tragically, when they do see him, they feel guilty at expressing this for fear of alienating their resident parent, on whom, as they see it, their security depends. They literally worry that they may wake up one morning and discover that their remaining parent has left. This is one of the most significant causes of night terrors, nightmares and being unable or unwilling to go to sleep. Each parent is thus led to the conclusion that visits by the non-resident parent do not afford much joy or comfort for the child.

'I used to arrive every other Friday to pick up my two boys,' says a divorced father. 'The atmosphere was always fraught. My elder son usually looked quite pleased to see me, although he would never be as bubbly with me when his mother was present as he was with me on our own. My younger son, however, sometimes did not even look up as I came into the room. I found it embarrassing, humiliating and deeply irritating. There would be their stepfather looking on, and I always felt that he was glad if they weren't all that excited by my arrival. On one occasion, the toddler, the child of my wife and the boys' stepfather, opened the door to me and shrieked, "Oh, not you again!" Where can he have picked that up? I don't believe that that was an original or spontaneous thought of his own, given his age. I was absolutely furious. I wondered if there was any point at all to my visits.' Research suggests, however, that there is, without doubt, considerable value to visits with the non-resident parent but that some children are reluctant to express their pleasure freely in front of the parent who is responsible for their day-to-day care.

Only one parent

Over half the children involved in parental separation or divorce worry a good deal about their resident parent, and this is another well-documented effect. They worry about her health and her wellbeing at every turn and they question, whenever she is ill or upset, whether or not she will be able to continue to be able to care for them. 'I felt very strongly that she was all I had in those years,' remembers one young woman whose parents split up when she was a child. 'I was very close to her and far less close to my father and his new family. I thought he would probably have me in with his family if anything happened to Mum, but I knew it wouldn't be the same. I felt in some way that I would only half-belong there.'

Do brothers and sisters help?

The elder child is likely to take the brunt of a parental divorce and is the one normally entrusted with more information than the younger siblings. Although children welcome information, they also experience with this a sense of greater pressure and responsibility. They feel that they have to be strong for their younger brothers and sisters. The youngest child often feels shielded by the fact of having older brothers or sisters. One recalls: 'I was the eldest girl of five. I was thirteen when my parents split up. All I remember is endless cooking and looking after the baby because Mum couldn't cope. Every time the baby cried, she started crying too. I stayed till I was seventeen, but by then I felt I had to get out. I do think I did my bit. I'm sure I would have done better at school if I had had time to do homework. But I was always doing things for my brothers and sisters. Sometimes they used to drive me mad: I remember one Saturday morning when I had just cleaned the kitchen floor and my youngest brother came in, covered in mud, and walked all over it. I made such a fuss that Mum came down to see what was going on, but she was in no state to do anything about anything.'

Generally, however, research shows that children who remain with brothers or sisters fare rather better: solidarity helps. For the only child, there is no let-up or escape route from the atmosphere at home. And, of course, there are other disappointments too, as this four-year-old girl's question illustrates: 'Why can't we have a baby sister, Mummy? I want a baby, Mummy. If Daddy came back, could we have a baby then?'

Being an only child can be a solitary existence, particularly so for a quiet, introverted child. Having a brother or sister, however, does not necessarily guarantee good company, as this teenager remembers: 'My father left my brother and me when I was two. All I remember of those early years is him beating me up, butting in, making me cry, stealing my toys. I don't know whether or not I provoked him, but he certainly wanted to make trouble. I just thought he was a wally. He's twenty-one now (I'm nearly nineteen), so he's calmed down a lot, thank God. And I must say that whenever we were in real trouble, we would stick together.'

Can children cope?

Monica Cockett found, in a study carried out for the UK's Health Advisory Service in Exeter, in which she looked at the needs of young people attending psychiatric and psychology services, that over half of these young people came from families in which they were no longer living with both their natural parents. It is now known that children who have experienced the loss of one parent through divorce are more likely to be among those referred to the psychiatric services.

People want to believe that they are doing the best for their children, that their children are intelligent, resilient, level-headed and thus, the thinking goes, they will 'get over it'. Most children do. However, some experience considerable emotional pain, fear and loneliness for at least two years and typically up to five years, and some for longer. Parents, as well as relatives, teachers and family friends, need to be aware of this, in order that each may offer the child the best possible support that she or he can provide, once it is established that the marriage is breaking up. No one should continue to assume that the child is not particularly bothered simply because she or he has not openly expressed pain.

We should reassess the still-popular belief, which was particularly prevalent in the 1970s and 1980s, that a good divorce is better than a bad marriage. It appears from much of the research that children have a far greater tolerance to their parents' poor relationship than to the loss of one of their parents.

Helping a grieving child

First and foremost, how things are organized in the short term tends to be consolidated in the long term. This is why it is so important that your child's lifestyle and your own do not descend into chaos at this time – vitally important.

You may well be tempted to say, 'Oh, I can't manage proper meals at the moment' or 'Getting her into bed on time is beyond me right now'. However, eating and sleeping must be the two top priorities, both for yourself and for your children. Never mind if the housework slips somewhat for a time, but at least feed the family and get the beds made. It will help all of you to feel better. It is distinctly depressing coming home to a place where the beds are unmade, there's a pile of washing-up in the sink and clothes are scattered all over the floor. Don't let things go, for your children's sake and your own. Just getting on with these basic routine tasks will make you feel better and you will have a more attractive home in which to live.

You will be prepared, having read all of this chapter, for your children to suffer with mood swings and at times to be extremely trying to you during a period when you yourself are least able to cope with them. Even though it is hard for you, you may have to keep reminding yourself that the separation was not of their making and not of their choice. It is more than likely that it was the last thing they wanted. You do, in these difficult circumstances, have to try to be endlessly patient and, above all, to be affectionate, loving and caring. You will need to offer your children continual support and reassurance that they are safe with you, that you will look after them and that you love them dearly. You will find that by treating your children in this way you will often succeed in defusing angry fits and tantrums and have the effect of making them want to behave lovingly towards you. Each of you can offer the other support.

You may, very naturally, feel angry with your partner – but beware of running him down to the children. They will find this very hard to take: it will create a conflict for them in that they love both of you and yet do not wish to alienate you by showing you that they also love your partner, when there you are telling them how bad he is, how he hasn't given you any money, how he lies, how he's unreliable and so on. Children need, deeply, to feel that they have a mother and a father whom they can love and who love them. Never, ever tell a child, 'Well, he certainly doesn't care about you,' however tempting and however true this may be.

Your children may experience problems in getting to sleep or with nightmares once asleep. They may well want to come into your bed. Whether or not you let them must be your choice. Some experts say that this is a bad habit to get into and should never be allowed, others state that it is not a problem in the short term and that the children will grow out of it. It's worth remembering that in some cultures babies and young children always sleep with their mother. Newborn and young animals are continuously by their mother's side, day and night.

Your children may need extra help and active participation by you with their homework, and of course this is important. Being unwilling to go to school is a problem that needs to be handled gently: ideally, you should take them there and collect them at the end of the day if they are still young. It will not help children to miss school, in either the short term or the long term, however distressed or unwilling they may be about attending. Once they are there, they will have the benefit of plenty of activities that will serve to distract them, if only for a short time, from their concerns with home.

Crying and being clingy are typical problems, it needs hardly be said, with children who are sad, frightened, disturbed and grieving for their absent parent. You may have been glad to see him go, but it is unlikely that the children are. They are actively grieving for their absent parent in very much the same way that we mourn someone who has died. Remember that children live in the present, always for the moment, so they are not capable of understanding that they will see Dad next weekend or next Tuesday or next month. Promises and arrangements for meetings at some time in the future have little real meaning for them. Comfort your children whenever they cry and reassure them with kisses and hugs. Never turn them away, however distressed or angry you yourself may feel. This is a profoundly emotionally demanding time for you and you will, of course, be drained at times. There will be times when all you can do is comfort your children and insist on regular meal times and bed times.

Now and again, think of inexpensive treats for your children to cheer them up. If the children are young, make fudge or shortbread, for example – both are cheap and fun to make. Try to take them for a walk in the fresh air whenever you can and at least once a week. You could take them swimming at the weekend, perhaps with some of their friends. They can express pent-up energy in this way and enjoy themselves, too. They will also benefit by maintaining their friendships. Treats do not have to be expensive: what children really like most is doing something grownup with you, like cooking or even a simply DIY job. Try to involve them as much as you can with the things you have to do, and make them fun for the children. No child wants to be told: 'Not now, I'm busy', and certainly not the grieving child.

Finally, don't be tempted to hold out false hope to your children, for it is important that they come to accept the reality of their new situation. If you are certain that your partner is not coming back, don't let the children think that he might, even though this is obviously what they want to hear. You need to help them towards a calm acceptance of their loss. This may take some two years or more, and this is perfectly normal. Many children need up to five years fully to adjust to the loss of a parent and some never adjust or only partially so. You are the one who can help your children the most, and with the most love.

TIME FOR YOURSELF: SEE YOUR FRIENDS

People need other people, and our emotional health depends to some extent on being able to meet this need. Human beings have a need for love and understanding and a need to love and understand others. Friends not only facilitate the two-way process of understanding and caring, they also make us laugh (the best release of stress and tension there is), they entertain, they expose us to new concepts and new experiences and, over the years, they share with us life events, achievements, disappointments, losses and successes in both our personal and professional life. Some of your close friends will prove a great source of strength to you at this time. Nearly everyone benefits greatly by having a few very close friends and a circle of less close friends: no one is an island.

5 Contact with both parents

One of the features of separation and divorce which disturbs most people who are witness to it is that the interests of the parents and children frequently diverge. Our society, and this is reflected in our legal system, contains an ethic that in such situations our children should be placed first . . . the links of parenthood may be hard to preserve once the parents have parted, but my argument is that we should do all we can to preserve those links as it is generally in the interests of children that they continue. (M.P.M. Richards, Child Care and Development Group, University of Cambridge, in the paper 'Post-divorce Arrangements for Children: A Psychological Perspective', published in the Journal of Social Welfare Law.)

The importance for a child of continuing an amicable contact with both parents following separation can hardly be over-emphasized, as a substantial body of research underlines. Many parents find this very difficult, however, and some find it almost impossible to achieve. In this way the child loses contact for ever with one parent. Even if, some years later, the child manages to re-establish contact with the absent parent, valuable time will have been lost, the relationship will be more difficult to re-establish and the child inevitably suffers. For these reasons it is desirable that contact starts without delay immediately after the parental separation and continues on a regular, not sporadic, basis.

There may be some confusion regarding the terms used by the courts and family lawyers about the arrangements made for children. In 1989 the Children Act was passed in the UK; it collected much of the law concerning children and families into one important piece of legislation. The Act emphasized the importance of parental responsibility whether families live together or not.

Before the Children Act, the courts would be likely to make an order about custody (now termed residence) and access, defined or undefined (now termed contact), and a maintenance/clean break order (now a maintenance, or Child Support Agency assessed, order if benefits are involved). These orders would be made whether parents agreed or not, and where there was a problem the court would take a decision and then make an order. Usually one parent was granted custody and made the day-to-day decisions. Sometimes a joint custody order was made, which meant that the child lived with one parent, but that the other parent needed to be consulted about major decisions. Although this arrangement was important to parents, it was not always helpful in practice and sometimes led to arguments about arrangements. Parents, particularly non-resident parents, are still inclined to think that once they leave the house they have no right to be concerned about their children's school, their friends and their everyday difficulties.

Although the law may vary slightly in other countries, most family lawyers and courts in the USA, Australia and New Zealand support the philosophy of an enduring and joint parental responsibility, and endeavour to promote co-operation between parents.

When parents are very angry with each other, it is very difficult to remember how important each parent is to the child. Contact arrangements work only when both parents support the arrangement. Some non-resident parents give up because they believe that they cannot fight the opposition from the resident parent, rather than because they have no interest in their child.

Since the Children Act was passed, the law assumes that both parents retain responsibility for their children when the family no longer lives together. The courts make an order for residence and contact only when parents cannot sort this out for themselves. Usually parents are able to make an arrangement with the help of their family lawyer and/or mediation services. When the problems between parents are more serious – if there has been violence and abuse – family lawyers are more likely to be involved in seeking the protection of the court.

What is mediation?

Mediation services have been available in the UK for at least fifteen years to help parents to sit down together, with an impartial third party (a trained mediator), and plan for their children's future. The Family Court Welfare Service, which is part of the Probation Department, can provide information about these services. Many family law firms provide an initial free half-hour appointment for parents, in which some of the confusions about the process of separation and divorce can be sorted out. There is at the time of writing (1966) a new Family Law Bill going through Parliament, which will mean more changes. Many parents will need to seek advice about the new arrangements.

In the USA mediation has been used for many years – the first family court was established in Ohio in 1910 – and provision varies from state to state.

Some fathers, and a few mothers, disappear from the lives of their children after separation. One or both parents often consider this to be in the children's best interests, although in fact it is unlikely to be so unless the departing parent was very violent or abusive to the children. The children themselves usually wish for frequent and regular visits with the absent parent, and research shows that this is, without doubt, in the children's best interests.

It is important to establish a pattern for contact visits just as quickly as possible. This should start directly after separation. Sorting out contact visits should not left until 'later' or turned over to solicitors to deal with. You, as the children's parents, should be able to make some sensible arrangements between yourselves in the best interests of your children. Remember that what is arranged in the short term tends to become established practice in the long term, so do give the arrangements some careful consideration at this early stage.

Research shows that children's relationships with their parents can change substantially following parental separation. The relationship with the non-resident parent becomes, predictably, less intimate as day-to-day contact is lost, and often more indulgent. While it might be supposed that the relationship with the resident parent, usually the mother, becomes much closer, this is not in fact the case. Studies have indicated that that relationship is also undermined and generally weakened. This is partly as a consequence of the resident parent assuming total child-care responsibilities, and thus becoming more authoritarian, and having less time and less money. It also reflects the fact that children may bear some resentment to her for having caused or encouraged the departure of the other parent.

Even when parents are able to make good arrangements, children will be likely to experience a change in their relationships with both parents. Both non-resident parent and children have to work harder at keeping in touch about things that they used to be able to take for granted, such as when a child does unusually well at school. Resident parents may need to work for longer hours outside the home, or require a more varied social life, and thus expect their children to become more independent. Parents may then see less of the children just at a time when the latter are feeling vulnerable. The children are also likely to blame one or other parent for what has happened, and this can cause confusion.

It is obviously important to be aware of these issues while making decisions for the children's contact times. 'Do you remember my name?' was one six-year-old boy's opening remark on telephoning his father, whom he had not seen for some weeks.

In a huge number of cases, one-third of the total, in which the mother has custody, the father is not seeing his children. As time passes, this one-third proportion gradually increases. Within just a few years of divorce, only a minority of children are still in contact with their fathers. One father sums up the view of many on this sad state of affairs as he comments: 'I can well believe it. I longed to see my children, but I dreaded picking them up from my ex-wife and her husband. I felt as if I were on trial. Taking them back, I couldn't wait to be shot of the place. I managed regular contact right through until they were old enough for me to buy them a car, but it was a struggle and I can well imagine some men would have thrown in the towel. It was desperately painful.'

The greater the effort that each parent can make to provide easy and regular contact for the children with their parents, the better it is for those children.

There are well-documented cases on record in which contact visits have become so impossibly strained, or have even been entirely prevented by the resident parent, that the absent parent has taken the law into his own hands. There are some 1,000 *known* cases of abduction in Great Britain every year, and some children disappear for ever, usually out of the country. Child-snatching is already a major problem in the USA, and it will only be by sensitive and sensible behaviour on the part of separating parents that we do not have to witness the same trend in the UK. Abduction, it need hardly be said, is usually deeply distressing for the child, the more so the younger the child.

In some cases both parents have been advised by their solicitors to remain in the marital home, despite the fact that the relationship has entirely broken down, until there is a legal resolution on the matters of residence, contact and finance. This is clearly not in the best interests of the children concerned and is therefore a situation that should be avoided if at all possible.

To conclude this discussion of the importance of contact for the child with both parents, the well-documented remarks made in the 1973 child access case, M *v.* M, seem appropriate:

> The companionship of a parent is in any ordinary circumstances of such immense value to the child that there is a basic right in him [the child] to such companionship. I for my part would prefer to call it a basic right in the child rather than a basic right in the parent. That only means this, that no court should deprive a child of access to either parent unless it is wholly satisfied that it is in the interests of that child that access should cease, and that is a conclusion at which a couple should be extremely slow to arrive.

What sort of arrangement?

The arrangement should afford the child enough time with his or her parent that the child can fall into a natural home routine with him. Brief visits to the park and the cinema do not give the opportunity to build a fulfilling relationship. Overnight stays should be encouraged, if these are possible and practicable.

The most common arrangement that parents settle upon is for the child to spend alternate weekends with the non-resident parent. There is a number of workable variations on this pattern, though, such as these:

- The child spends four days of every week with Mum and then moves to Dad's for the next three days, or *vice versa*.

- The child spends every weekend with the absent parent.

- The child spends one day each weekend with each parent.

- The child alternates weekends with each parent.

- The child spends one weekend each month with the absent parent.

- The child sees the absent parent only during the school holidays, for extended periods, and not at all during term-time.

- The child sees the absent parent not by regular arrangement but through either the parent or the child making irregular and sporadic requests for contact.

Split weeks

While contact with both parents is undeniably important for children, each child needs to have a clearly defined home, a secure base, from which they can explore the world and get to know the absent parent. Split weeks can work well for some children and this arrangement ensures close and continuing contact with both parents. Conversely, split weeks can have the effect of making the children feel that they do not really belong in any one place. The children will have to make constant adjustments to their lifestyle, as no one home is exactly the same. The children may feel that their loyalties are seriously divided between the two parents and this undermines their sense of security. When their lives are organized in this way, the children are subjected to many more leave-takings, and there is research to show that some are unhappy with this type of arrangement for contact.

Every weekend

For the child to see the non-resident parent every weekend may suit some parents quite well, but it does not appear to be in the best interests of the child. Every weekend with Dad, for example, means that the child never spends leisure time with Mum. Mum is responsible for getting her or him to school, helping with homework, enforcing bed time, doing washing and so on, but she never gets the chance to enjoy a day with her child – perhaps at the seaside – nor can she take the child to see the maternal grandparents if they live some distance away, for example.

The child may feel dissatisfied with the arrangement in that she or he misses Mum at weekends, never has leisure time to spend alone at Mum's home and will not be able to see friends unless Dad happens to live close by. However, in common with all relationships, if it works, it works: if the child is happy spending every weekend with Dad, then that clearly is the best solution for contact arrangements.

KEEPING IN TOUCH

Both the children and the absent parent will benefit by keeping in close touch, in addition to enjoying each other's company during contact visits.

- **As the resident parent, encourage your children to telephone and write little notes to their absent parent as often as they wish.**

- **As the absent parent, write to your children often and never overlook birthdays, Christmas and other special occasions.**

- **Keep in touch with their schools so that you are invited to open days, sports days, parent-teacher evenings and so on.**

- **Never ever let your children down: if you say you will be there, be there; if you promise something, make sure that that promise is fulfilled.**

One day each weekend

Spending a day and a night with the non-resident parent and returning to the resident parent for the remaining day of each weekend works well for some children.

Every other weekend

Spending every other weekend with the absent parent has become a common pattern for child contact following parental separation. Some specialists are unsure about the reasons for this and question whether or not the arrangement is as sound as it is believed to be. Twelve days with Mum and two days with Dad: is it psychologically healthy for the children? Is it fair to both parents? Unhappy parents make for unhappy children, generally speaking.

The arrangement is good in that it is regular, but twelve days may be too long a period from one contact to another for a child if that child is to maintain an easy and relaxed relationship with the absent parent. It is certainly too long for many absent parents.

Think for a moment about any other close relationship: would you yourself be able to build a very deep and close relationship with someone whom you saw only on alternate weekends? Would you yourself be able to maintain a close and loving relationship with someone with whom you have lived but are now committed to seeing only every other weekend? Do you think that the relationship would be weakened by this loss of contact?

Contact every other weekend makes a lot of sense for the two parents, and this is undoubtedly how the arrangement has evolved

ENJOYING YOUR SOLITUDE

There will be times when your former partner is looking after the children when you, as the resident parent, find yourself unaccustomedly alone and in need of company. This is the time to recharge your batteries and enjoy a respite from non-stop child care. Be sure to keep in close touch with your friends, particularly in the early months of separation, and take the first few steps towards making a new life for yourself.

and why it continues to be accepted by many families, but it is my belief that there should be telephone contact and one or two brief visits (a couple of hours, perhaps) with the absent parent during the intervening twelve days.

This additional contact may help the relationship with the absent parent become more natural. Twelve days in the life of a three-year-old, after all, is a long time. At this young age the child has to experience the sorrow of parting but is not yet old enough to understand what is meant by 'See you in two weeks'.

It is known that children under five are at greater risk than older children after the loss of a parent by divorce. This is by no means to suggest that older children do not suffer. They do, very considerably. A child of less than five, however, is muddled and incapable of understanding the reality of the situation. For small children short periods of time, perhaps not even overnight stays, with their father, depending on how much care the father has given the child when the parents were living together and provided that the parents are able to co-operate very closely, may be best. Short, frequent visits with the non-resident parent may work out better for the young child.

One weekend per month

Many parents have to accept the one-weekend-per-month arrangement if the absent parent lives some considerable distance away, but it is less than ideal for the child. The absence of one parent for twenty-eight days in the life of a child is significant, for all the reasons stated above regarding visits every other weekend.

Only during the holidays

For many contact with the absent parent during the school holidays is the only practicable arrangement that can be made. If the absent parent lives in another country, for example, holiday contact is really the sole viable option. In these cases contact is, ideally, extended to several weeks, so that the child has the opportunity of re-establishing and consolidating the parental relationship. The child should be given the opportunity of making contact by telephone and letter with the resident parent throughout this extended period with the absent parent, and, conversely, with the absent parent during term time.

Sporadic, irregular contact

Irregular contact with the absent parent is usually distressing and unsatisfactory for the child (if not for the absent parent, too) and, for the child's sake, should be improved upon. It is, without doubt, in the child's best interests that close and continuing contact should be maintained if at all possible, unless there are serious reasons why this should not be so. (Violence and child abuse, for example, are obviously grounds for considering the question of ceasing contact.) Children flourish best when they can rely on contact arrangements and know when they will next see their other parent. 'I don't even know Dad well enough to argue with him,' says one child who sees his father only occasionally.

Special occasions

The child's birthday, Christmas and other special occasions are, typically, the events that cause the most discussion between parents over contact. Naturally both parents want their children for birthdays and Christmas. Some parents elect to take it in turns, year by year. Others find that the resident parent generally has the children for important events such as birthdays and Christmas.

Once they are old enough, children should be encouraged to express their own wishes about which parent they would like to be with. Children often decline to give their own opinion, however, for fear of alienating one or other parent: 'I'm eleven years old. I'm a child. And you're asking me to make decisions that adults should make. It's not fair.' Even when they do state what they want, it's likely to be a tactful compromise, in even quite young children: 'We'd like to be at Mum's on Christmas Day. We can come to you on Boxing Day.'

New Year's Eve can quite frequently become a bone of contention: the resident parent will claim what she sees as her right to have the children over Christmas and will offer the non-resident parent contact with the children for several days before Christmas and again for New Year's Eve and New Year's Day. This means that the non-resident parent has to prepare for the children's Christmas a week earlier than anyone else, spend Christmas alone and is denied the joy of adult celebrations over New Year's Eve, unless of course he feels sufficiently secure in the children's affections to arrange for a babysitter for the evening. Little wonder that parental discord tends to surface at this time of year.

If the children's wishes are to be put first, it is probably best to let them choose. If they do not wish to make the choice, then alternating, year by year, seems the fairest way.

What children want

'We never see enough of Dad. It's quite a long drive to his place and as soon as we've got there we have to come back home again.'

'My Dad lives in another country, a long way away. I haven't seen him for ages.'

'Mum left when I was twelve and she went to live abroad. I go and see her in the holidays. I really look forward to seeing her. I would like to see her more often.'

'I wish they would live here in the same home, like before. We could all be together.'

'I ask him to buy me a gift whenever he comes to see me . . . yes, he does, usually.'

'I like it if he takes me to a football match.'

'He is very serious. Sometimes I get quite bored.'

'I *hate* it when he's late. Mum gets very cross. Then he gets cross. It makes me cry.'

'Sometimes he comes too early for me and Mum makes him wait outside. I don't like that.'

'I know it's Mum on the phone, because his voice goes cold and he says, "Yes. Yes. Yes. OK. Bye".'

'He came to visit us and shouted at us, so I don't want to see him again.'

'She will say one time that she never wants to see her Dad again and another time that she wants to see him, so she's ambivalent, but it obviously plays on her mind.'

'Everything is all right as long as I don't let Mum and Dad speak to each other.'

'Dad lives just round the corner so I can see him whenever I like. I like that.'

'I can't go to my friend's party, because it's my weekend with Dad and Mum is going away for the weekend. It's not fair.'

'They should have asked *me* when I wanted to visit.'

'Why can't I change the visiting times myself?'

It's clear that children want some degree of autonomy, flexibility and regular contact without conflict between the two parents, and it is to be hoped that this is within the capability of each parent to organize for their children. How not to conduct contact visits is, perhaps, best illustrated by a case described by Wallerstein and Kelly in *Surviving the Breakup*:

> Six months after the separation, Marty talked angrily about his father and how the visits were always 'screwed up'. 'It's not worth going any more . . . I don't have any fun anyway.' From his mother we learned that Marty not only used to anticipate visits eagerly, but was the primary agent in setting up the visits. He called his dad often to suggest get-togethers, but his father always had excuses. Marty told us of the day his father arrived to take him on an eagerly awaited trip some distance away. The meeting time had not been clearly set, and Marty was playing at a nearby friend's house. In a rage, the father blamed Marty's mother for sabotaging the day's outing and left without him. When Marty came back ten minutes later and learned his dad had taken his sibling and departed without any effort to call for him, he was devastated. He sobbed for fifteen minutes, receiving little comfort from his outraged mother. Soon thereafter Marty developed his protective veneer, acting noncommittal whenever the father called. In talking with us, Marty's interest in seeing the father was evident, but equally strong now was his need to save face by pretending it all did not matter.

This is a clear-cut case of neither parent behaving as the child would wish, their own mutual hostilities and emotional baggage being allowed to dominate the child's right to uncomplicated contact with his absent parent. It should be added, however, that even in cases where there is conflict between the parents, children still fare better than those who have no contact at all.

Giving up

Many parents feel that it would be very much easier for them if their former partner simply disappeared and left them to get on with looking after their children on their own. This view is frequently expressed by the resident parent: they see the absent parent as nothing but an irritation and as someone who upsets their children, and them, every other week. The absent parent is typically no happier with the situation either. These are some of the views expressed by separating parents:

'She never has them ready for me on time.'

'He always turns up early to pick them up and late to bring them back.'

'If I don't carry on seeing them, I won't have to pay any more.'

'His cheques are always late, but he doesn't seem to realize I still have to pay the bills. If he's not careful, I'll stop his visits.' Yet, if contact is maintained in a helpful and friendly way, financial needs are more likely to be met.

'He always brings me back their dirty clothes to wash . . . why should I?'

'She seems to think that I'm her unpaid babysitter and I just go and pick them up when she feels like going out – that's not what it's about.'

'He can have them for a change – serves him right.'

'He didn't even ring on her birthday – so I'm not going to let him see her next weekend.'

'I'm not taking them – why should I? If he wants to see them, he can come and get them.'

'I can't let them go on seeing him. It upsets them too much.'

'I'd forgotten how wonderful it was to be able to have time without the children for a bit – and even to go away for the weekend.'

'She keeps waltzing in, bringing them presents, and I'm not left with enough to buy them shoes when they need them. It's absurd.'

How many of these statements appear to be made with the child's best interests in mind? Very few, it seems. It is a lamentable fact that separating and divorcing parents tend to put themselves first.

Why do non-resident parents give up?

- Some parents believe that it is in their children's interests to disappear and that continuing with contact can only upset the children.

- Some believe that neither parent has the opportunity to make a new life for themselves if contact visits are maintained – in some cases for fifteen years or more.

- Some simply lose interest in their children, perhaps because they have never got to know them properly, perhaps because they were not deeply committed to having children in the first place.

- Some believe that they will not have to pay for child support if they no longer participate in visits.

- The resident parent makes it so uncomfortable for the visiting parent that he eventually gives up the battle. Some mothers elect to take their children out when the father is about to visit. Some tell them point-blank that they cannot see their children. Some mothers insist on accompanying young children, especially if they are under five, on the visit to the absent parent's new home, which makes it difficult, if not impossible, for the child to detach him or herself from Mum and establish a relationship with Dad.

- The journey is so great, one or other parent having moved away, and so expensive and time-consuming to make that the non-resident parent gradually loses touch, with visits becoming more and more infrequent.

- The children themselves reject the non-resident parent.

- The non-resident parent remarries and has children, and his older children are compelled to take a back seat.

- The resident parent remarries and she and the stepfather present a united front of continuing hostility to the visiting father.

It is for these very reasons, which cause parents to regard contact visits with sadness and hostility, that many professionals who are concerned with families at the time of family breakdown are currently trying to bring about reform in the divorce laws. It is believed that it is the traditionally adversarial nature of matrimonial proceedings, where fault has had to be proved by one partner against the other, that has brought so much hostility into child-care arrangements following separation and divorce. It is increasingly thought that by reforming the divorce laws, eliminating fault as grounds for divorce, parental attitudes to contact between their children and their former partner may, in time, gradually become less harsh and confrontational and start to focus on the interests of the children concerned.

Mediation services can play an important part in encouraging parents to work together to plan for their children's future.

'I don't want to go'

It's not unusual for children to say that they do not want to see their absent parent for a variety of reasons. More often than not, they are fine when their parent comes to collect them. Sometimes, however, they genuinely do not want to go, in some instances just on that particular occasion, but other instances they do not want to go at all.

In some cases children are attempting to reinforce their security with their remaining parent by evincing no interest in the absent one. In some cases, however, children are genuinely hostile and angry with the non-resident parent for having, from their point of view, deserted them.

It is fair for children to enjoy flexibility as well as continuity of contact and thus it is perfectly reasonable for a child to elect to go to a friend's party rather than see his or her parent. Both parents need to be flexible and accommodating in such circumstances as far as is possible. It is, of course, easy for the non-resident parent to imagine that the other parent has put the child up to the idea of not going and for another row to flare up. Clearly, such situations can be avoided if both parents act reasonably.

If the problem appears to be more serious, and the child does not wish to have contact at all, although both parents favour it, it may be worth going for family therapy or mediation services (see Useful addresses at the end of the book).

Can contact be damaging?

'Everything's OK as long as I don't let them talk to each other,' commented a nine-year-old girl daughter of divorced parents. A few specialists believe that contact with the non-resident parent is not just unimportant but actually damaging unless the parents are on friendly terms. They maintain that the resident parent should control all contact. There is little evidence to support these opinions, and certainly the great majority of specialists working in this and related fields subscribe to the belief that it is *loss* of contact that is damaging to children. The open hostility and anger expressed by separating parents could indicate that contact is potentially harmful to children, but the evidence appears to show that while children can tolerate conflict, they cannot easily deal with the loss of a parent.

Other arguments can be used as evidence that contact is damaging. These include the fact that neither the children nor the parents are given a decent opportunity of making a new life for themselves, without the absent parent; the fact that children of divorcing parents are in danger of becoming spoiled as each parent goes to greater and greater lengths to lavish presents and treats upon them which, ultimately, afford the children little joy; the fact that, almost inevitably, one parent (usually the non-resident one) is seen as wonderful (too indulgent) and the other as strict (too authoritarian and busy); and the fact that the children have to make constant adjustments in order to accommodate the different life-styles they encounter in each of their parents' homes.

On balance an enormous amount of research material exists to show that the belief that contact is damaging is mistaken and very little to prove that it is harmful.

Encouraging contact with the absent parent

First and foremost, separating parents are experiencing one of the worst periods of their life: it is well worth remembering that everything gets better in time. In the same way, over time, visits become part of a pattern that every member of the family accepts. Gradually, the hostility between parents diminishes. Soon children come to accept their visits to the absent parent as an integral part of their life. All the problems of the early days gradually resolve.

Some absent fathers discover that they have more to offer their children than they realized, and enjoy activities with them with which they did not bother to become involved when they all lived in the same home. Many fathers remark how much closer they have become to their children since the divorce. This is clearly some-times the result of being solely responsible for looking after and entertaining the children, when before this would have been carried out by the mother alone or by mother and father together. While this is clearly the case with fathers who have sons, some girls, too, have found that their relationship with their father has improved since parental separation.

For those who experience insurmountable difficulty over contact between the children and the absent parent, contact centres have been set up in a number of towns (the organizations in Useful addresses at the end of the book will be able to provide details of the one nearest you). These centres are designed to help parents who have nowhere suitable of their own in which to entertain their children for a visit, parents who have to travel long distances to meet their children (both can meet at the contact centre), and parents who have as yet been unable to resolve their emotional difficulties sufficiently to be allowed unsupervised contact. The centres can also be used as a neutral meeting ground to help those families in which the child (or baby or toddler) wants to see the father but is too young, or unwilling, to leave the mother. Contact centres are typically equipped with a playroom with toys, a kitchen and a team of volunteer helpers.

Putting the children first, and this we must do, means helping to ensure continuity and flexibility of contact with both parents. Children regard their natural family as their permanent one. Their new relatives – step-parents and their families – can become very important to children, but they do not replace the importance in the children's mind of their own natural mothers and fathers and their own natural grandparents. While mothers may be able to deal successfully with the loss of relationships with former relatives such as their husband's family and accept that these are now not part of their present lives, children sometimes find this very difficult as their attachment to grandparents can be very strong. In the same way, for children, the absent mother or father will always remain of utmost importance and that relationship will always be present in their minds, whether they have contact or not, and will always have a powerful influence on them. Continuing contact with the absent parent is, undeniably, for the sake of the children, an important principle of separation and divorce.

6 Lightening the burden

'I just couldn't help myself . . . although I knew it was wrong of me. Whenever he brought them back, I'd interrogate them, as subtly as possible, under cover of getting their tea and in between the splashing around at bath time. I just couldn't bear to think of them away from me, with him, enjoying a so-called natural family atmosphere like they do with me. We should all have been together . . . that's what the children wanted and that's what I wanted too.'

The emotional burden for children of having two parents living in two separate homes, in some cases many miles apart, has been fully explored in earlier chapters of this book. This chapter is concerned with how we may lighten the burden for our children as they make the regular switch from one parent's household to the other.

It is a natural consequence of separation that parents gradually grow apart and become, in many senses, less like each other and with little in common. This distancing naturally provides more scope for arguments and differences of opinion over how the children should be brought up and how contact visits should be managed.

The resident parent may have a lot more to cope with than she/he did before the separation and this alone can lead to the children feeling less secure than before. You will find that the children's stability can be strengthened by drawing them into helping with the day-to-day running of the household. Obviously, some things take longer to do when you involve the children, but the emotional benefit, to all of you, is worth the effort.

'Now, let's see, what shall we have for supper? What do you think? Come on, I need your help.' You can make your children feel valued in this simple way and help to build up their self-esteem and renew their self-confidence. You may be surprised at how quickly your children will respond in a positive way to this type of approach.

You may find that your children quite quickly become more mature and more considerate by thinking about some of the problems you have to cope with day by day. Ask them to help by all means, involve them fully in family and domestic life, but do beware of over-burdening them. For example, take care not to make them anxious about any money worries you may have. Children need to believe that the next meal and a roof over their heads are unquestionable certainties in their life. Never, for an instant, let them suspect that you are worried about being able to pay the mortgage or the rent, or to buy food. It is reasonable, however, to refuse them those treats, outings, clothes or holidays that you cannot afford: don't lose sight of the fact that parents who remain together also sometimes have to refuse their children's requests. Being unable to pay out the best part of £100 for a pair of top-of-the-range trainers, for example, is not necessarily a consequence of separation. You can point out, if necessary, that the situation would not have been any different if Mum and Dad had stayed together.

You may find as time goes on that your children will become calmer and better adjusted to their new lifestyle and soon some may volunteer their help where they perceive it is needed. Several research studies show that resident parents rely a great deal on their children, in particular adolescent girls. One survey noted that some parents, several years after their divorce, acknowledged that they would not have made it at all without the help and support of their children. It is worth repeating, however, that you should take care not to over-burden your child with adult worries with which they cannot possibly help.

Discussing visits to the other parent

Without being needlessly inquisitive or succumbing to jealousy, it is worthwhile discussing with your children, in general terms, their visits to the non-resident parent. It is quite natural to ask what they did, what they ate and whether or not they enjoyed themselves.

Remember that children live very much in the present and they may not be particularly forthcoming. That does not matter. All you need to do is to show a friendly interest in how they have spent their time with their other parent and to give them the opportunity, should they need it, of airing any problems that they may have with their visits.

The child as go-between

The following quotations illustrate how children of separated and divorced parents are sometimes used as go-betweens:

'You'd better ask your Dad for new shoes. I certainly can't afford them.'

'When you see your Dad, tell him I need some money. There's no way we can carry on managing as we are.'

'We're coming to you for Easter. Mum's going away with her new friend.'

Putting the onus on the child to carry unpalatable news is simply unfair to the child. There is no reason whatsoever why the child should be burdened in this way – passing on news, experiencing the reaction and passing back the reply which, in turn, may provoke a further reaction. These sorts of issues should be dealt with in an adult fashion by the two parents alone during a meeting, on the telephone or by letter, in whichever way seems the least likely to provoke anger, jealousy and guilt.

In families in which there is more than one child, using the children as go-betweens can be damaging in that it may lead to emotionally harmful rows between the children themselves, should they elect to take different sides.

The chief aim of a child visiting the non-resident parent is to cultivate and enjoy a loving, happy relationship with that parent. Nothing should be done by the resident parent to undermine that important aim. Equally, the non-resident parent should refrain from criticizing what he deduces of the children's new lifestyle at home from the occasional glimpses he catches. This constitutes a rather more subtle use of the child as a go-between. It is, in effect, a way for the parent to express anger about his former partner to the child with the – possibly unconscious – aim of undermining the partner's relationship with the child. It can, of course, be very difficult for parents to achieve this ideal standard, but this is what should be aimed for.

Blanking out their other life

Some separating parents make a point of showing no interest at all in the relationship that their children develop with each partner. They maintain a false friendliness at collection and departure times or, worse, an icy coolness in which suppressed hostility is barely concealed. These attitudes are less than helpful to the children learning to accommodate to the fact that their parents now live apart and to adjust to two different lifestyles. For the sake of your children, do try your best to show that you genuinely approve of the contact they have with the other parent, that you welcome it and that you will do your best to facilitate it, even though you may find this difficult to do.

Watch what you say

You need to think carefully before you speak, bearing in mind that your children may unwittingly (or knowingly!) repeat your words to your former partner. Children often select information to relay to either parent in a desire to please, but it may turn out to have the opposite effect. It is, of course, very difficult to be on your guard at all times. Simply keep to yourself those matters that you regard as highly personal and anything that you consider would anger your former partner.

Where to go and what to do?

Wallerstein and Kelly found during their research for *Surviving the Breakup* that:

> The part-time parent and the part-time child often begin with a bewildering sense of no place to go and no idea of what to do together. The relationship is from the outset beset by practical problems: by the presence of children of different ages and colliding interests; by the

absence of the mother who had often served as an interpreter of the children's needs. To many fathers these practical problems seemed at first insurmountable. What to do with young children still in need of actual nurturing care? Or with older children who appeared to need continual stimulation and entertainment in order to control their restlessness? Some confused men changed their entire routine for the children's visits, others changed nothing at all, and still others, equally perplexed, expected the children to take full responsibility for the agenda. 'I feel like a camp director,' said one exhausted father.

Positive attitudes

Your children may continue to wish for many years that you and their other parent had stayed together. They may continue to hope for this even after your marriage to new partners. Bearing in mind your children's feelings and the importance for them of happy contact with both parents, these attitudes may help:

- There is always more than one point of view on any matter. Don't expect your former partner to see things in the same way you do.

- Both parents need to continue to function in relation to the children as a *team*. When you are both present, reassure the children about the things that worry them.

- Try not to draw too much on your children's feelings – you should avoid seeming frail to them as far as this is possible.

- Answer all their questions honestly, openly and without rancour. Be as natural and open with them as you can. Do your best to communicate with them and work through their feelings and fears with them.

- Avoid the temptation to prove to the children that you were right and your partner was wrong. Don't go over old history.

- Start learning how to let go. You can no longer control your children's time with your former partner. Your children have the right to enjoy this time and be nurtured by it.

- The time between visits can seem very long to a child. Encourage your children to have brief, interim contact, if only telephone calls, between visits.

- Don't expect things to be *fair* – life isn't always fair. Try to remember that good contact is of inestimable value to your children both in the short and in the long term.

- Don't read too much into what the children say about their visits. Bear in mind that children may feel that they have to keep secrets and should not show that they enjoy the company of the other parent for fear of alienating the parent who looks after them for most of the time.

- It is inevitable that the children will be subject to different lifestyles and different rules in their two homes: accept it.

- Each of you will spend more concentrated time with your children than you did before the separation. Some of this is time that you would have spent with your partner. This can be enriching, especially in these early days. It would not be helpful, however, to become too emotionally dependent on or needy regarding your children: they need *you*. Ideally, for this reason, avoid introducing a new partner into their lives for the time being if you can. Children may find the introduction of a new partner very difficult to accept in the early days of parental separation.

- Your consideration for your children and their long-term health, ideally, will help to alleviate any resentment and bitterness that you may feel for your former partner.

- Above all, be consistent!

New surroundings

When your children visit you, as the newly absent parent, in your new surroundings, you may expect them to be very curious about it all and to question you closely. Answer them as fully as possible and do everything you can to reassure them that you are getting used to your new room/flat/house and that you enjoy it, although, of course, you miss them very much. Your children may worry about you in your new home and you can do much to lessen their anxiety on this score at least. Show them the good points about your new home and gloss over any disadvantages. Show them where they will sleep if they are to stay over and where their toys and books can be kept. Encourage them to establish their own territory within your new home so that they come to feel part of it and, in this way, continue to feel part of you. This particularly applies to young children: teenagers will naturally have a wider perspective, although they, too, need their own space within your new home and will not take kindly to being made to feel like guests. One of the best compliments your children can pay you in this new alien situation is to show you that they regard your home as their home – with, of course, the natural disadvantages, with which you will already by familiar, that this brings, such as loud music and belongings strewn around!

Some newly absent parents have very unsuitable accommodation in which they can provide very little for the child. This, naturally, can cause difficulties between the two parents, with the resident parent saying that the children cannot stay. Many absent parents are compelled to take their children on outings because they have nowhere suitable to pursue normal family activities.

A natural, homely atmosphere

Remember first and foremost that your children have come to see you yourself. You do not need to impress them, to lavish treats upon them or to keep them occupied with games and outings every minute of their stay with you. That is not to say, of course, that you can just sit back and read a book and let them get on with amusing themselves – you do need in some senses to be one jump ahead.

The experience of a woman who went out with a divorced father of two children is significant: 'I remember being at his house one Saturday when the children, to whom he was very attached, were visiting. He was playing a board game with them when a friend of mine arrived: she had come from Manchester to London to see me and meet him. She came in the front door, which opened on to a tiny sitting room, which is where we were, with him and his children taking up the whole sitting-room floor. Well, he just didn't move, didn't greet her, didn't offer to take her coat or anything. It was bizarre, I had to step across him and somehow squeeze her into the room. I introduced them all, but he still didn't say a word. He was so intent on "entertaining the children" that he simply could not cope with anything else. She happened to be a psychologist and counsellor – and she found it pretty odd, too. It was as if he was frightened of anything coming between him and the children. He was practically fixated on them. He never became more relaxed, I have to say. I don't know how this came over to the children or what they made of it all.'

The secret is to make some concessions to your children's visits but not to be so intense with them that the relationship becomes an emotional burden to them. Your children will welcome becoming part of your new life and being encouraged to meet your new friends and socialize with them. At the same time, however, you should remain sensitive to their needs. You may feel, to start with, that if they are to stay over, you should have done all the food shopping and made up the beds before they arrive – but this isn't necessary. Children like to be considered as part of your home and, at the beginning at least, they will be fascinated by your local shops and your local supermarket and will derive pleasure in being allowed to choose some of the things you buy to cook with them. Don't forget: these are not house guests on whom you have to make a good impression – they long, long ago formed their impression of you and this is unlikely to alter substantially. Simply be welcoming, show them that you are happy to see them, hug them, be warm to them. Remember that they will feel a little uncertain at first when they see you in your new home. It will feel much more strange to them than it does even to you. They are used to seeing you as 'Dad' together with Mum at their first home. This new situation is quite novel for them.

You will probably find that small children establish their own little world for themselves in their absent parent's new home quite quickly. Some of the things they bring with them, some favourite toys, for example, they will probably be reluctant to leave at your place. But the things that you buy for them, on your new territory, they will probably be pleased to leave with you as this clearly signifies that this is their space and that they are coming back again. With further visits you can gradually increase and consolidate their sense of security in this way.

When it comes to meal times, encourage your children to help in any little ways that they can. This is all part of making them feel 'at home'. Even quite young children can set a table, wash and peel potatoes and help with making simple puddings; and they will enjoy it. They are unlikely to see these things as chores, to start with at least.

You could consider suggesting to them that they might like to keep a pet of their own once you have settled into your new home. They will almost certainly be pleased and excited by this. Let them choose, within reason, what they would like to have. Bearing in mind that you will have to look after whatever it is that they choose when they are not in residence, hamsters, rabbits, guinea pigs, caged birds and fish are all quite easy and straightforward to care for. Cats are easy and very independent, provided that you live in an area where a catflap is a sensible option. A dog clearly requires a greater commitment from you yourself. You will have to walk it twice a day, and it would be unfair to leave it on its own all day while you are at work. When you are away, you would have to hand it over to a trusted friend to look after and take for walks or put it into kennels. Small children are, however, often perfectly content with something no more demanding than a hamster or a gerbil, and they are quite capable of feeding and watering it themselves and of cleaning out its cage.

In order to consolidate and strengthen your relationship with your children, it is important for all of you that they feel relaxed with you in your new home. Remember that it is your children's second home. With this in mind, encourage them to invite their friends to drop in, if they don't live too far away, and have parties on or around the time of their birthdays and at Christmas. It is important to encourage this type of atmosphere at your home when your children are young, for otherwise when they are older they will quite naturally see less and less of you as they become more independent and more absorbed by friends of their own age and less dependent upon you for their wellbeing. You don't want, if you can avoid it, to lay the foundations for a situation, when they are older, in which they tell you that they cannot see you this weekend because they are going to a friend's party on Saturday night. There is no reason why they (and their friends, too) can't get ready for the party at your place, making a number of telephone calls as well, no doubt, and have you collect them from the party so that at least you spend Sunday with them. Remind yourself that just because they want to see their friends, it does not mean that they do not wish to see you. Be glad for their sakes that they are making strong social relationships: this is how it should be. Children of separating parents may find it harder to socialize and make new friends and to keep their existing friends, so do everything you can to facilitate their friendships.

TABOO SUBJECTS BETWEEN YOU AND YOUR CHILDREN

- How rotten the other parent is.

- Many problems – never let your children feel that their home may be taken away from them or that there may not be enough money for food. Don't torture yourself with thoughts of the luxury items that you cannot afford: many other people cannot afford them either, irrespective of whether or not they are separated.

- Criticisms of the other parent's lifestyle.

- Sex when it involves either or both parents or new partners of either parent.

Routine matters

Children feel safer and more secure if their normal routines are adhered to. This applies to what they eat and when they eat, when they do their homework, how much television they are allowed to watch and at what time they are expected to go to bed. It's natural enough that there will be differences between their two homes, but you will know enough of their pre-separation routines to make life easier for them in these respects. Major changes are very difficult for children to adjust to. A whole range of additional lesser changes may seem overwhelming to them.

Discipline is one area that can become a highly charged focus of discontent between the two parents, and here you must listen to your own voice. Only you can set the rules for what you regard as acceptable behaviour from your children: if these standards differ from those of your former partner, you could explain to them that Dad likes it this way, Mum likes it that way, and that no two people hold the same views.

Children of different ages

A divorced father of four children between the ages of two and fourteen says: 'At times I find it remarkably difficult to master all their different needs without the help of my former wife. I'm still at the stage of changing nappies for my young daughter, while my teenage son wants me to collect him from a party at two in the morning!'

Younger children will require a lot more looking after, on a practical level, than a teenager, and it may be that you will all benefit by arranging for the children to visit at different times. However, this can lead to sibling rivalry and jealousy, and the older children will not be on hand to help with the youngest. Try different variations and see what works best for you, your children and your former partner.

Remember that each child will want her or his own space and to be able to spend quality time with the absent parent. In addition, adolescents may require more emotional attention and time from both parents than younger children.

Playing off one parent against the other

Children may try to play off one parent against the other to get their own way. 'Mum lets me stay up for this programme – why can't I with you?' and 'Dad's got me a telly for my bedroom: can I have one here, too?' are questions that will be familiar to some separated parents. Again, you will have to explain that no two people hold the same views and that what you have decided is for the best in your view, but that doesn't mean that you don't love the child as much as the other parent.

It's very easy for separating parents to fall into the trap of looser and looser discipline and more and more presents. This is positively harmful for the children and encourages them to think of love exclusively in material terms. Try not to spoil your children, for this will otherwise become a downward spiral, which will ultimately be emotionally damaging.

In some situations, in which there is already conflict between the parents, the giving of presents and the relaxation of any rules and discipline can become a horrible point-scoring exercise, with each parent trying to outdo the other in vying for the children's approval. Guilt-induced behaviour such as this puts emotional and financial demands upon the parents and may affect the healthy emotional development of the children.

Listen to your own voice

Wallerstein and Kelly, writing in *Surviving the Breakup*, recorded the results of their research, which showed that parents should follow their instincts:

> Although the wishes of children always merit careful consideration, our work suggests that children below adolescence are not reliable judges of their own best interests and that their attitudes at the time of the divorce crisis may be very much at odds with their usual feelings and inclinations.
>
> One unexpected finding which emerged serendipitously in our search for norms was the dividing line between those children in the first three grades and those in the fourth to sixth grades in their

responses to the family rupture and in their relationships with both parents. Psychological theory, while recognizing the continued developmental progress of the child, does not shed light on some of the significant attributes of children at the threshold of adolescence. The long-lasting anger of children in the nine-to-twelve-year-old group at the parent whom they held responsible for the divorce; the eagerness of these youngsters to be co-opted into the parental battling; their willingness to take sides, often against a parent to whom they had been tenderly attached during the intact marriage; and the intense, compassionate, caretaking relations which led these youngsters to attempt to rescue a distressed parent often to their own detriment have led us to rethink our expectations of these children. Furthermore, their particular age-related propensity to split the parents into the 'good parent' and the 'bad parent' (which was often at odds with the role of the respective parents over the years and which seemed to be rooted primarily in the children's own acute fears) led us further to doubt their capacity to make informed judgement about plans which would be in their own best interests. These observations, and the fact that several of the youngsters with the most passionate convictions at the time of the breakup came shamefacedly to regret their vehement statements at that time, have increased our misgivings about relying on the expressed opinions and preferences of youngsters below adolescence in deciding the issues which arise in divorce-related litigation.

He's keener now that he's left

A father may become a better parent after he separates from his partner. Whereas before he was often working and left child-care matters to his partner, the father may now have sole responsibility for looking after his children when they visit. Some men find that they can offer their children a more positive and involved commitment than was possible before. Now they are able to focus upon their children and their needs in a way in which they could not before the separation.

Diminishing intimacy with their children is exceptionally difficult for some men to accept, and those fathers who do, against the odds, maintain contact with their children experience more bitterness, depression, alienation, loneliness and suicidal feelings than those who simply give up. Keeping in touch when there is opposition from the resident parent requires determination and resilience. Contact should be actively encouraged by the resident parent and by friends and other family members. Most of the research shows that good contact benefits the children (and the absent parent) greatly.

Research also indicates that the children's relationship with the newly absent parent can change dramatically after separation. The hitherto unconcerned father can transform himself into a model of good parenting after divorce, while a father who, before divorce, was apparently happy and committed, may eventually turn his back on his children, much to their consternation and anguish. The resident parent, therefore, should try not to be surprised or angry at witnessing such a change, for this is not unusual.

Goodbyes are always tough

One of the inescapable tragedies of separation and divorce is that parents and children frequently have to say goodbye to one another. This is never easy either for child or for parent. The resident parent often finds that she misses her children when they are away on a visit, and the non-resident parent can become bitterly depressed by what he sees as the injustice of having lost his children through the collapse of the marriage.

If the children are very young and the parental relationship is good, perhaps at the end of the visit the father can put the children to bed back in their first home. This will help the children, although it could awaken powerful feelings of misery and unexpressed anger between the two parents. It is helpful to the children to see their parents getting on well, and therefore, rather than just dropping the children at the end of the visit and leaving, it would be better if the non-resident parent were to enter the house for at least a few minutes, even if it is not possible to stay for a cup of tea or a drink with the other parent.

Research shows that the better the levels of contact with the absent parent, the more likely he is to pull his weight in respect of money, support and general help for the family. Children who continue to have good relationships with both parents are those least affected by separation and divorce, while those of openly conflicting parents may find it harder to adjust and accept their parents' separation. If the everyday matters are handled well, some children of divorced parents will become adults who are more resilient, better decision-makers and more mature than those of their peers who remain within their original family.

7 Their future in your hands

'When Dad left, I didn't want to go to school any more. I didn't want to see my friends and have them asking me questions.'

Your first priority has to be arranging your children's visits to the non-resident parent. Once the visits are slowly becoming established, you will naturally start to consider the other major issues that may surface during separation and divorce. These may include:

- Your children's physical and emotional health.

- Who is responsible for looking after the children during school holidays.

- Social matters that relate to the whole family.

- The question of new partners.

- Contact with both sets of the children's grandparents.

- The resident parent deciding to move abroad.

- One parent deciding to move away.

- The children's education.

- Financial matters and the division of property and other assets.

- Employment.

- Child care.

- A new will.

Your children's health

The physical and emotional health of your children is almost bound to reflect what is going on in their life. Parental separation and divorce significantly increase your children's chances of falling ill or becoming psychologically upset, as described in earlier chapters. Both parents can reduce the stress imposed on the children by their separation by showing an understanding of what the children are suffering, by keeping conflict to a minimum and away from them, and by each parent actively encouraging a happy and harmonious relationship between the children and the other parent.

This was the experience of a father of two children: 'It was about five years since my first wife divorced me and I had continued to see my children every other weekend for an entire weekend ever since. The visits were OK, but they were not without their problems. I shouldn't think my first wife would have minded if I had never showed up again. But what really got me down was the strain the weekends imposed on me and my new wife, together with the fact that my children did not appear to me to be getting much out of their visits. They were ten and eight at this time. They fought continually between themselves. They would be withdrawn when they arrived on the Friday night and it would often take all of Saturday for them to settle in. Come Sunday they had to leave again. In the end, I suggested to their mother that I should see them for one weekend each month rather than two. Unbeknown to me, she immediately put this to my children, whereas I intended to suggest it to them myself. I mentioned it to her first only as a courtesy. Anyway, the children themselves vetoed the suggestion and said that they wanted to continue with their fortnightly visits . . . and that's what we did. I wouldn't say that the quality of the visits necessarily improved, but I felt better in that the children had made it clear that they wanted to see me, no matter what she thought, and she knew that. That did make things easier for me: I felt I was on firmer ground.'

Very few parents find that visits are entirely without problems, but bringing up children always poses problems, irrespective of whether or not the parents are separated. Visits can sometimes be very challenging, but it is important to persevere with them for the sake of the children and, indeed, of the absent parent, too.

School holidays

If the resident parent does not work, school holidays do not present such a great problem. The absent parent may have the children to stay for at least a week, if not two weeks, during school holidays, with the resident parent taking care of them for the remainder of the holidays. Some parents are able to organize the holidays so that they can share the holiday time, but this is not always possible.

If the resident parent works, clearly some compromise has to be reached between the two parents. This is bound to involve either time or money, or both. Each parent can elect to work shorter hours during the school holidays in order to accommodate looking after the children, or they can invest more money in child care. Neither offers a perfectly satisfactory solution, and neither is always possible. In some families one of the grandparents may be able to look after the children during the day until the resident parent returns from work. Friends may be able to help out now and again, but this is unlikely to be a workable arrangement for the duration of the long summer holidays. This is one of the issues which you and your former partner need to get on to a firm basis in order to give your children stability and security.

Social matters

Your life as a single parent may be more rather than less sociable, even though this social life is likely to include your children and your friends' children, as going out may now be more difficult to organize. Do encourage this, for good friendships are important to children, particularly during parental separation when their own friendships may flounder. Never be too proud to accept invitations and to accept offers of help: take them as the compliment they are intended to be.

New partners

The interests of parents and children are often not the same when the question of a new relationship arises and it helps children if an introduction to a new person in their parents' lives can be made gradually and sensitively. Frequently, however, the marriage has floundered because of the existence of a third party. In the case of the absent parent, she/he may have already moved in with the new partner so that the children, inevitably, meet the new person right from the start.

These are important points to consider:

* **Children do not give up the idea of their parents reuniting for many years.**

* **Children take, on average, about two years to get over the crisis period of parental separation and a further three years (or more) fully to accept it.**

* **Children who have lost one parent fear losing the remaining parent.**

* **Many children simply tolerate their natural parents' new partners without actually liking them.**

The issue of new partners is discussed at length in Chapters 8 and 9.

The children's grandparents

It is a sad fact for grandparents that some lose touch with their grandchildren entirely. If the mother is the resident parent, the maternal grandparents will probably be visited as often as they were prior to the separation. It is the paternal grandparents who are more likely to lose out, and many of them feel this very keenly. The absent parent may already find it difficult enough to manage visits with his children without the additional strain of building in a joint visit to his parents with his children as well, particularly if the grandparents live some distance away.

Grandparents and in-laws may be keen to offer help with the children and their involvement is important to the children's sense of identity and continuity.

Mother moves abroad

'I lived in Cuba for many years with my husband and daughter. The marriage was over for a long time before I had the courage to leave. I knew that if I left I would not be able to return and he would be unlikely to be able to visit me here. The decision, then, was one of absolute enormity: I had to recognize that I was depriving my eight-year-old daughter and my husband of seeing one another ever again, at least until she was grown up.'

In some families the resident parent, usually the mother, like the one quoted above, may want or need to move a considerable distance away, thus making it virtually impossible for the absent parent to visit. Some of these cases have come to court. The prevailing belief is that the mother has the right to pursue her career and live where she wishes even if, in so doing, her child or children are deprived of *their* right to a relationship with their father. It is possible that this attitude may change, given the increasing concern for the children's best interests.

As research shows that one in seven of all single-parent families are headed by men and that there are no great differences between those looked after by men and those looked after by women, the father (usually the 'absent' parent) in such cases may wish to consider becoming the resident parent, thus allowing his former partner to pursue her career or choice of where to live but without her children.

There is no easy solution to this complex set of circumstances, and each separated family has to work out together what is best for their children. Will the children have comparable educational opportunities in the new country? Will the children be able to make friends easily? Do the children speak the language? Parents should consider together to what stresses and difficulties, both short term and long term, they are subjecting their children.

One parent decides to move away

While it is relatively rare for the resident parent to decide to move abroad, it happens more commonly that either the absent or the resident parent finds it necessary or desirable to move away from what used to be the area of the family home.

If the parents cannot agree arrangements for the children to travel, the court may be obliged to intervene, but it is often more difficult to keep the children in touch with both parents. If parents are living at a considerable distance away from each other, arrangements for contact may change to provide for longer stays at less frequent intervals.

Social and economic changes in society mean that some fathers are as available to look after their children as mothers and many prefer to do so. Some women are prepared to leave their children with their fathers while they follow their own careers and see the children at weekends.

The children's education

As separated parents grow away from one another, and their feelings and beliefs diverge, significant differences concerning education and, possibly, health, too, may emerge. The man who once steadfastly supported comprehensive education may now, as the absent parent, find himself inadvertently backing a minor public school for his sons. Although he knows that he has let his children down, he wants the best for them even more now that he is no longer in residence. Conversely, the woman who herself enjoyed a public-school education now elects to send her child to the local school 'because her friends are going there and she'll be happy, and she can walk home safely'. Economic factors, obviously, also play an important part in educational decisions.

Circumstances change and people's attitudes and priorities change, so don't assume that your former partner has elected a form of education for your children solely in order to annoy you. She/he probably has valid reasons for the choice, and it would be helpful for both of you to discuss your reasons calmly and to come to a considered decision that puts the best interests of the children first.

Both parents should see the children's school reports, if possible, and both are entitled to attend parent-teacher meetings, sports days and other events to which parents are invited. Your children need the involvement and interest of both parents in their education. Children feel supported if both parents share a concern for their progress at school and recognize its importance.

Financial matters

A significant percentage of separating couples will not have resolved the financial issues before their divorce (or at least their decree nisi) is granted. This is messy, of course, and serves only to increase stress and, possibly, bad feeling. The financial issues should, ideally, be sorted out efficiently and quickly through mutual discussion, negotiation and agreement. Recourse to the courts can result only in there being less to share both for you and for your children.

The financial arrangements that have to be made when parents separate are often complicated and very much bound up with issues about the children, and with parents' feelings about each other. For many families there is very little money to divide between two, now separate, households.

Traditionally, each parent has sought legal advice from a family lawyer, in order to obtain the best financial settlement for themselves and to safeguard their future. Increasingly, family lawyers are adopting a conciliatory approach, based on the resources of the family and the needs of the two emerging households, each of which will want to provide in some measure for the children. The cost of protracted court proceedings will reduce the amount of money available to both parents. Even if parents are eligible for legal aid, if there are assets, such as the family home, legal aid fees will have to be repaid once the house is sold, and before the capital can be divided. If the family did not own its own home, only matters of tenancy have to be resolved.

Mediation services, referred to in earlier chapters, are available in most cities and towns in the UK and provide an opportunity for both parents to sit down together to look at ways of sorting out the problems concerning their children. Comprehensive mediation services will assist parents to sort out all financial issues, as well as the children's problems. These services work with both parents, each of whom is encouraged to obtain the advice of her/his own solicitor and to cut down the amount of time spent in separate negotiations and resulting conflict. The lawyer will offer advice and support, while, with the assistance of the mediators, parents make informed decisions for themselves.

The division of assets and income will be based on the needs of both parents and the children. The past, present and future working opportunities of both parents will be taken into account.

The Children Act 1989, and the Family Law Bill, which is currently being debated in Parliament, place an emphasis on parental responsibility, and the court will now make orders concerning your children, your property or your financial support only if, as parents, you are not able to reach an agreement with the help of your lawyers or the family mediator. Working together in this way is not easy, especially when parents have lost faith in each other and have little trust that the plans being made will be carried out. The courts will, however, have a greater expectation that parents will retain an adult and continuing responsibility for their children and will place the onus on parents to make constructive plans for their future. Family lawyers and mediators will continue to provide the expertise and support, while parents will retain joint responsibility for the decisions taken.

In the USA, Canada, Australia and New Zealand there have been similar moves to make the end of marriages less antagonistic. Governments are now aware of the research message that, when parents fight, it is much harder to protect children from the harmful effects of parental separation. While some countries are ahead of the UK in legislation for planning less adversarial divorce, there is still debate about how best to assist parents, and solutions offered vary.

The family home

One of the most difficult problems for parents, if they are joint house owners, is how to organize the living arrangements for both parents without moving the children from the familiar surroundings of home. Usually, a large part of the family assets are tied up in the house. If there is sufficient capital and income available, one parent can sometimes agree to buy the other out or to delay the distribution of the capital until the children are older or circumstances change. Sometimes the splitting of the family resources means that there is insufficient money to maintain the house, so inevitably it has to be sold. Often the non-resident parent will not be able to buy a new home without the release of capital tied up in the house, but parents are sometimes able to agree that the children's needs come first, and the sale can be delayed. The poor state of the housing market and negative equity problems, at the time of writing, have not helped separating parents. Naturally, children would usually prefer to stay in their home and, although they can see a move as an adventure, many parents and children find it an added stress.

Financial matters naturally vary with each couple, but broadly, the following topics have to be considered:

- **Property.**

- **Joint possessions.**

- **Cars.**

- **Life insurance policies.**

- **Shares.**

- **Pensions.**

- **Inheritance.**

The division of assets will reflect the earning power (current and potential) of each partner. Maintenance for a non-working resident parent will be considered, but cannot be assumed to be granted automatically. The major earner can expect to pay maintenance for the children until their education has been completed, as well as school fees if applicable. The cost of child care, if both parents are working, should also be taken into account.

The resolution of the financial matters can, regrettably, cause very considerable stress and friction between separating parents, often to the detriment of the children's wellbeing. As a parent you obviously wish to do the best that you can for your children's financial security, but you may sometimes have to remind yourself to stand back and calm down in the interests of their physical and emotional health. Protracted and acrimonious disputes over money and property can cause damage to *both* parents' relationships with their children.

Legal fees can quite easily run into thousands of pounds. In a long-drawn-out dispute, involving court appearances, these fees can amount to tens of thousands of pounds. The temptation to work out anger and revenge through the negotiations for the financial settlement may be overwhelming, but it should be observed that agreements made voluntarily between the two parents, perhaps with the assistance of a professional mediator, and subsequently ratified by the courts, work out very much cheaper, and less emotionally draining, than those outcomes determined by the courts.

It is wise to seek professional legal advice at as early a stage as possible. You should check to see whether or not you are entitled to legal aid: not many people are these days. You may also find it helpful to read *The Divorce Handbook* by Fiona Shackleton and Olivia Timbs. Consult, too, the Useful addresses section at the end of the book for further sources of information and advice.

Finally, courts very seldom alter the children's place of residence. They normally simply confirm what the arrangements have been up until now. If moving home can be avoided for the children's sake, this is undoubtedly in their best interest. If a move appears to be inevitable, at least allow as long a time to elapse as is practicable between the departure of one of their parents and the move from their familiar home.

Employment

Normally, both parents will continue working as before, with such child-care arrangements as are already in place continuing. The non-working mother, however, may be compelled to consider taking a job, or resuming her career, in the foreseeable future. This will, of course, require child-care arrangements to be made and paid for. Non-working mothers are no longer automatically awarded sufficient maintenance to live on for the rest of their lives.

Child care

Arrangements can be made with a registered childminder, a live-in or live-out nanny, an au pair, friends or family members such as a sister or one of the grandparents of the children. Each option has its different drawbacks and different costs. You should enquire as to the range of costs and take this into account if you are considering resuming work following divorce. Talk to as many friends and acquaintances as you can in order to determine what options for child care exist in your area. If you wish to continue being a full-time mother, you could make a case for this, based on the undoubted value to the children of a fully resident parent, particularly children who have already lost one parent, and on the high cost and potential unreliability of child-care arrangements.

If the resident parent is the mother who has remained at home to look after the children, both parents will need to consider whether or not this is possible after separation. Most parents understand that too many changes for children in those who look after them are not easy for them to accept. So, if the resident parent needs to consider taking a job for financial reasons, it may be possible to delay this while the children are very young or for a part-time arrangement to be made. Maintenance payments usually take into account the need to consider the children, but they also allow a degree of flexibility for the order to be reassessed when circumstances change.

Making a new will

During the period of separation, before divorce, you should consider the contents of your will. Amendments may need to be made. If you were to die before divorce, without having made a will, the rule of intestacy may provide for your estate to be divided in a way that you would not wish.

When you draw up your will, you should also nominate, with your former partner's agreement, the person or persons whom you would wish to see appointed as legal guardians to your children in the event of your death.

If there is likely to be inherited money coming into the family from either parent's relatives in the near future, parents sometimes want to consider this not only in the financial arrangements but also for their children in the future. The family lawyer or mediator may want to include this along with discussion about making new wills.

Big decisions

The decisions that you make at this time will undoubtedly have far-reaching and long-lasting implications both for you and for your children. Consider the long term as well as the short term.

Most family lawyers now base financial settlements on the balance between the assets and the needs of both parents. Mediators will certainly use this as a basis for negotiation. Difficulties between parents on financial matters often arise when circumstances are altered, either by the remarriage of one or both partners, or by altered financial status. Often parents cannot settle their differences without help, but the same underlying principle will apply concerning the flow of assets and need. Parents who are able to retain a charitable view of each other's circumstances will find it easier to make fair adjustments between themselves. Unfortunately, renewed bitterness about financial matters can affect arrangements for the children which have been working well. It is, therefore, in the interests of everyone to deal with each new problem with as much understanding as possible.

By no means all settlements are worked out by lawyers, mediators or the court. When parents work out an arrangement between themselves, they will usually ask their lawyer to check it. Even when these arrangements seem workable, they do not always endure in the long term unless parents are able to adapt to the changes in their own and their children's lives.

If you secure a settlement that is so financially harsh to your former partner that she/he is left with a sense of rancour and alienation, your children may ultimately suffer. Do not be tempted, on the other hand, to waive a reasonable amount of maintenance for your children just because you wish to end your financial dependence upon your former partner. You will almost certainly regret this grand gesture.

If you, as the major breadwinner, are the one making financial provision for your children, satisfy yourself that the amount is fair and reasonable. If it is not, both you and your children may ultimately suffer. There is nothing to be gained, with the children's best interests in mind, by making such a mean settlement that hostility from your children's resident parent is likely.

Once these big issues are resolved to each partner's satisfaction, the relationship between the two of you as the children's parents is likely to improve. So, in turn, will your children respond and benefit by this. Don't forget, during all the stresses of separation and divorce, that familiar routines are of great value to your children. Keep up regular meal times and bed times, make sure that they see their friends and that visits to relatives carry on as before. Visits with the absent parent should be maintained as a most important priority. If the children seem upset about going on a visit, bear in mind that this probably reflects the fact that they are anxious about leaving Mum, not that they do not wish to have contact with their father. The visits should not be cancelled or postponed, even though this may avoid distress in the short term. In the long term, the children will undoubtedly benefit by establishing a good relationship with their absent parent. Both parents will consequently benefit, too.

8 Daddy's girlfriend and Mummy's boyfriend

'I didn't want him in the house, he wasn't really interested in us and he kept arguing with Mum and bossing us around. I wanted Dad back – I kept asking him but he said it was impossible.'

Children typically react to the loss of one of their parents from the home with shocked disbelief, fear and sometimes panic. Many children, if not most, take some time to recover from this considerable psychological trauma. The matter of introducing a new partner to the children needs, therefore, to be handled with considerable psychological skill and empathy.

Many children long for the absent parent to return and continue to live in hope that this will happen. The introduction of a new partner, in theory, dashes their hopes – although many never really give up the fantasy that their natural parents will eventually be reunited and the family will be re-established as the children knew it before the separation/divorce of their parents.

You should satisfy yourself as far as is possible that the person with whom you start a relationship is suited to you and is likely to be a good partner both for you and for your children. Much misery could be averted if all of us followed this apparently simple advice, but, of course, we sometimes find ourselves attracted to a clearly unsuitable partner.

Think analytically about how compatible with one another you are likely to be and think, too, about your reasons for selecting this particular individual. Beware of the need for *someone* as distinct from this particular person.

Are you compatible?

'I suppose if I had thought about it properly, I wouldn't have married him in the first place,' said one woman of her first husband. 'We had different political backgrounds, different religious backgrounds, different interests and we also engaged in extremely heavy rows. But the making-up was so sweet and so full of promise for the future that I carried on, driven in a sense. I failed to see what my sister was trying to tell me, which was: "What you have got now is what you have got – things won't change just because you get married. They'll be the same." She was more or less right.'

All the potential incompatibilities in the following list are surmountable, but, if they exist, they need to be carefully considered and, if there are too many, you need to think very seriously about your future. These are some of the issues you need to consider in order to decide whether or not you and your new partner are truly compatible:

- Do you confide in each other? There will naturally be some things that people prefer to keep to themselves, but a good relationship is normally open and honest. Deception and deceit are not part of a healthy relationship.

- Do you enjoy being with your partner? This may sound like a strange question, but in fact many people survive their relationship only by spending as much time apart as possible – through work, friends outside interests, for example. Are you compatible enough to enjoy spending some of your spare time together?

- What happens when you argue? Do you discuss real issues and problems openly and quickly resolve them? Or do you find that you squabble and argue a lot of the time, often about nothing in particular? Are you aware that there are some big issues in your lives that you cannot discuss at all without a major row?

- Do you find that your relationship sometimes gets into difficulties as a consequence of your different backgrounds? Or are the cultural differences between you a positive factor in your relationship?

▧ Do you respect your partner's intellect? Is she/he more or less bright than yourself? A reasonably good match is important if you are to remain compatible.

▧ Are your political views compatible? This may not sound all that important while you are enjoying the first stages of love and attraction, but political differences tend to emerge and assume a greater importance the longer the relationship continues.

▧ Would your religious beliefs cause conflict between you if you were to decide to have children together? How would the children be brought up – in your religion or denomination or in your partner's? Again, this may not sound like an overwhelmingly important issue in the initial stages of a relationship, but it could become a major focus for conflict and disagreement.

▧ Do you share a similar sense of humour?

▧ Is your sex drive compatible with that of your partner? Again, any differences between you may become more marked with the passage of time.

▧ Are you generally physically compatible in your appearance? Are you each about as attractive as the other?

▧ Do you consider your temperaments to be well suited? Do you tend to get on each other's nerves?

▧ Do you have shared interests – are there hobbies that you enjoy together?

▧ Do you ever consider ending the relationship – do things get so bad that you can imagine life without this partner?

- Do you agree on where you are to live, both in the short term and the long term?

- Do you like eating the same sort of things? Is either of you a vegetarian? Is either of you bound by religious constraints in your diet?

- Does your partner have irritating habits? Do you feel the same about smoking and drinking? Are there things about your partner that you cannot stand? These may become even more irritating as time goes on.

- How do you handle money matters between you? Does your partner strike you as extravagant, or mean, or irresponsible? Do you generally agree on how money should be spent?

These questions are intended to highlight any differences that could eventually come between you. They should show up possible seeds of discontent. You may find it interesting first to consider the questions long and hard in relation to your new partner, and then to take another look at the questions with your former spouse in mind. Could you have spotted the warnings signs had you known what to look for? Would you be able to avoid making the same mistake twice? Is your current partner clearly more compatible with you than the former? Some of the questions concerning compatibility point up very important issues, upon which relationships can founder. It is sometimes difficult to judge at the beginning of a relationship, but for your child's sake as well as for your own sake it is vitally important, this time, to be sure that you are embarking on a relationship that promises to be strong rather than another that may end in separation, with all the trauma that this promises, not only for you but for your children too.

Is there room?

Some experts believe that children cannot easily welcome a substitute parent into their lives while their natural parent lives. They consider that children will find it difficult, for example, to accept their mother's boyfriend, or eventually a stepfather, while they are maintaining contact with their natural father. Other experts disagree with this and point out that children, just like adults, can maintain a large number and variety of different relationships. Their relationship with their absent father will quite naturally be completely different from their relationship with their mother's new partner. It is likely, too, that a child will more easily accept a parent's new partner provided that they have continuing contact with both their natural parents and are in this way reassured that they will not lose either parent. The absent parent often fears that he will be replaced by his former wife's new partner, but this is unlikely to happen unless he himself stops visiting the children, thus creating a vacuum in their lives. Equally, children do not usually view a stepmother as an alternative to their real mother.

The right reasons

When you are thinking of embarking on a relationship, it is worth questioning yourself closely about your reasons, as any relationship you undertake will naturally have some effect and some influence upon your children: 'Well, he ran off with her, didn't he? So I thought he might like to know how it feels when the boot's on the other foot. Anyway, it was him that suggested I should see this man – apparently he's always liked me.' Tit-for-tat relationships and those formed on the rebound from a collapsing marriage cannot be said to be made on a sound basis. It would be wise to try to avoid acting in this way, particularly with your children in mind.

After the end of one relationship, most people will benefit by resisting the temptation to jump into another one: everyone needs time in which injured feelings can recover, pain and anguish can recede, and thought can be given to the reasons for the collapse of the marriage. Although it is tempting to believe that a new relationship will help to make you feel better, because you have been hurt, you may not be thinking clearly and a time for reflection can often be of more benefit than starting a new relationship, which will require emotional energy, too soon.

If you are embarking or considering embarking on a new relationship, it is most important that you do so for the right reasons. The following four quotations illustrate some of the wrong reasons.

'I was happy when I was married. I was simply content. I would have done anything for her. I used to give her all my money. I just need to find someone now to settle down with. And I hate sleeping on my own – I just don't sleep as well. And there would be someone to do the washing and ironing. I'm OK with cooking: I like that.'

'I can't manage the children on my own. It's simply a nightmare. I would never have had four children if I had thought for a moment that the marriage was not going to last. Right now, I need someone around the house, to help with odd jobs, to help keep the boys from running amok, to look after me and to bring some money in.'

'He lived next door and we got on quite nicely and we were both lonely, and that's how it happened. I must say with hindsight I would rather I still had my own place . . . but he's here now.'

'When I finally left my husband, I had nowhere else to go except to my lover's. Obviously, I took the children. It was all very difficult. They had never met him before. He had no idea really of what he was getting into: he didn't have children of his own. The first year or so was very difficult indeed – there were lots of rows and sulks from the children. He tried hard, but sometimes they really pushed both of us to the limit. When their father came to take them out, they would become completely over-excited, and when they came back they would be tearful and sulky and foul to both of us. If I could have known what it was all going to be like, I do wonder whether or not I would have made the same decision.'

Introducing the new partner

As illustrated by the case above, it is sometimes not possible to introduce the children to the new partner in a sensitive fashion over a reasonable length of time, although that is obviously the ideal if it can be so arranged. Ideally, have your partner meet the children for no more than a couple of hours to start with – for tea perhaps, or to go out for a burger. Don't make a big issue of the meeting. Allow the children space and time to make their own decisions in an unhurried way about the new person in your life rather than encourage hostility by presenting them with too strong an approach in the beginning. All they need to know at this early stage is that this is a friend of yours whom you would like them to meet. Ideally, for the first few meetings, choose some neutral territory rather than your home or your partner's home. The more relaxed you can be about introducing your partner to your children, the more likely it is that the children will accept your friend. However, it is essential to remember that your child's relationships and feelings cannot be determined by your own. Children have a right to their own feelings. If they do not like your new partner, therefore, this is their right: it is not really appropriate that anyone should attempt to persuade them to revise their views. It is to be hoped, over time, that they will come to see that you yourself are happy with this person and that they will be able to accept your partner into the new family circle.

The importance of introducing the children to your new partner over a considerable period of time, in as casual and friendly a manner as possible, can hardly be overemphasized. Don't let the children feel that they are being overwhelmed by this new person or that she/he is in any way a replacement for their natural parent.

You should, if at all possible, acquaint your former partner with the new state of affairs in order to prevent a situation in which the children themselves tell your ex during a visit.

Learning to recognize jealousy

Jealousy is defined as being suspicious or fearful of being displaced by a rival: and this is exactly what your children may dread. Having already lost one parent, they may fear what will happen to them when either parent introduces a new partner. They may be afraid that you prefer being with this partner to being with them and, consequently, that they may lose you as well. If you are the absent parent, your children may fear that their visits may cease now that you have found yourself a new friend. They may react by becoming more obviously attracted to you, more emotionally dependent on you and more possessive of you than they were before the arrival of your new partner. You can expect a lot of questions from your children about your new friend, questions that they put to you in order to allay their innermost fears. If you are able to reassure your children, which may take time, and recognize that their feelings of jealousy are an entirely normal response to the new situation, it may be possible to avoid the worst effects of the resulting insecurity and unhappiness that they can sometimes experience. Children may react in this way if they feel worried that they may lose a parent.

You should also be prepared for your new partner to feel jealous of your children. In addition, your new partner may feel insecure about your own relationship with the children. This may be expressed through criticisms of your being too soft with your children, of letting them get away with too much, of spending too much time with them (in other words, not enough with your partner), or spending too much money on them, for example. These criticisms may be valid – only you can know if they are – but, generally speaking, such statements tend to reveal more about the speaker than about the subject. If you are experiencing this sort of criticism about your children, stop to consider whether or not they contain some truth, and try to give your partner the attention she/he evidently seeks. This is a matter that is best discussed openly with your new partner, with attempts made together to try to sort out the problem. Sometimes, however, it is not possible to reassure both your children and your new partner and, if you perceive the jealousy aroused by your children to be abnormal or unwarranted, reconsider just how important this relationship really is to you. Is she/he worth it?

Keeping it alive

Starting a new relationship with inquisitive children in proximity is never going to be as easy as it would have been without them. However, remember that children can enrich a relationship as well. Show your partner that you care in lots of little ways that don't take much of your time but do show that you have not forgotten about her/him through the demands of your children. Spontaneous hugs and squeezes can do much to allay adult jealousy and insecurity. Ring your partner at work now and again to show that you care. Don't be so busy and so taken up with your children and your work that she/he starts to feel you wouldn't notice if she/he wasn't there at all. Send a card now and again – a funny one or a loving one –

to show that you are thinking of your new partner. Place a note in an unexpected place for her/him to find some time later. Balancing a new relationship with children is undeniably a difficult juggling act, but it can be done, as many people can testify.

Coping with your former partner's new love

Here are five divorced people's views on their ex-partner's new relationship:

'I left her for another woman, so it was me that caused the breakup of the marriage, but if I am honest I have to admit that when I found out my wife was seeing someone else, I really hated it. I couldn't bear to think of her with him in what had been our house . . . you can imagine . . . I can't put it more clearly than that.'

'I divorced him some time ago and I remarried. My ex's relationship with the woman he left me for had long ago finished. But then he met someone else. At first, I liked her, if only because she wasn't the other woman. But, after a while, I felt she was muscling in on us, trying to organize visits with the children and so on, trying to please them, and I felt very threatened. I was secretly aware, although I could not admit it at that time, that I still had feelings for my ex and I didn't really want him to have a girlfriend. I didn't want her looking after my children when they went to visit him.'

'He says he's got two Dads, which is ridiculous, *I'm* his father.'

'The idea of him in bed with this other woman is physically painful for me: I can hardly bear it, I find it disgusting. I just don't understand how someone could go from one person to another so quickly . . . it makes me wonder if he ever loved me at all. Was it real?'

'She left me for this other guy, leaving our son with me, I'm glad to say. But it didn't work out for them and she's on her own now. I don't know if she's happy, but she's made her bed and she'll have to lie on it.'

There are not many people who simply don't care what their former partner does with the rest of her/his life. Many people reveal anger, guilt, a sense of betrayal and even remorse, in relation to their former partner's new lover. These feelings are compounded, of course, by the fact that there are children involved and the children will be party to the new relationship and will, almost inevitably, be influenced by the new partner or partners. Few natural parents welcome the advent of what they see as their own replacement. It is not very likely, however, that their children will see these new people in their lives as substitute parents, unless the natural parents actively encourage this by disappearing from their children's lives. Children maintain a very special and irreplaceable relationship with each of their natural parents: substitutes won't do. It is much more likely that the children will form an independent and different sort of relationship with their parent's new partner: more of a deep friendship, at best.

Because of the potential for feelings of anger and guilt on the part of your former partner towards your new partner, it is wise to tell her/him of your new relationship – 'I'm seeing this person; we get on quite well' – as briefly as possible. Many parents feel compelled to add 'She's/he's good with the children too – they like her/him,' but far from soothing the former partner, this kind of remark tends to inflame old jealousies and long-dead feelings when it should, in theory, reassure the former partner that the children are happy. In this kind of situation, in which the emotions can still be aroused, many people find it difficult to remember to put the children first.

Thinking of the children

The following points may help in combining your role as parent with the introduction of a new partner in your life and consequently a new adult in your children's lives. These guidelines are in the best interests of your children, and thus in your best interests, too, when you are embarking upon a new relationship:

- Don't exclude the children from activities in which they were included before the advent of your new partner.

- Don't try to send them to bed a couple of hours earlier than usual because you want to be alone with your new lover.

■ Always defend them should the occasion arise. Don't laugh at their mistakes in front of your new partner.

■ If you are the absent parent, don't include your new partner in your children's visits to start with for more than a couple of hours at a time. The children may well feel: 'He can see her any time, but we've only got the weekend'.

■ Don't flaunt the sexual nature of your relationship. Avoid being too demonstrative with one another in front of the children, for they will surely be jealous and fear losing out on their parent's affections to a rival.

■ If your children have been used to coming into your bedroom whenever they wish, you may need to consider how to continue with this once you and your new partner have decided to sleep together.

■ Don't allow your new partner to take over the rules and the discipline of the home in relation to your children. They will not welcome this. You should retain your position as their authority figure, thus helping to engender a sense of stability and continuity.

■ Never make unfavourable comparisons between your former partner and your current partner in front of the children.

■ Don't undermine your former partner in any way in front of your children: they may eventually very well resent this.

Don't make the same mistake twice

Although it may be difficult, it would be constructive to try to take an objective view of the reasons for the breakdown of your marriage so that you can understand and accept it and so that you can do your best not to make the same mistake twice. This may help you understand what happened more clearly and will assist in the process of acceptance of the end of a very important relationship. Thinking about the events that led to the breakdown of your marriage may also have another important function. It may help you to consider a new relationship with more caution and with a better understanding of the difficulties that can arise. Many of us are almost unwittingly attracted to the same type of person, with similar faults, over and over again, so this is, perhaps, more easily said than done. The more aware you are of the dynamics of your former relationship, the less likely you are to repeat the pattern.

If your former partner was violent or cruel to you or to the children, look for the warning signs of this in a prospective new partner. If your former partner was reckless and irresponsible with money, be alert to the signs of this in a new partner. Beware, however, of being so sensitized to particular faults that you overlook other, potentially more serious ones that you may not have encountered before. You owe it to your children not to bring them into contact with someone who could be potentially damaging to them. They will already have suffered substantial trauma through the separation of their parents, so really try to consider their needs as well as your own.

Drinking too much

One of the most common causes of marital breakdown and of violence in the home is addiction to alcohol. When relationships break down due to violence there may be an association with drinking problems for one or both parents. It is often very difficult for those closely involved to be able to recognize when the drinking habits of a partner become a cause for concern. Can you distinguish between a normal, social drinker and someone who has become dependent on alcohol?

Alcohol dependency syndrome consists of seven essential elements, which psychiatrists and other doctors use as the basis of diagnosis:

1   The feeling of being compelled to drink.

2   A recognizable pattern of drinking – starting at roughly the same time each day and drinking approximately the same amount.

3   Drinking assumes priority – over health, family concerns, home, career and social life.

4   Altered tolerance to alcohol – increasing tolerance of drink is a significant sign of increasing dependence, but in the late stages of dependence, tolerance decreases and the alcoholic becomes drunk after only a few drinks because the levels of alcohol in the bloodstream are persistently high and the body's ability to deal, with the inflow of alcohol is impaired.

5   Repeated withdrawal symptoms – notably tremors (the shakes), agitation, nausea, retching, sweating, hallucinations (seeing and hearing things), fits.

6   Relief drinking – a drink on waking up to relieve the withdrawal symptoms.

7   Return of the familiar pattern after abstinence – someone who is severely dependent is likely to return to her/his former drinking pattern within a few days of ceasing abstinence.

Physical disorders include liver malfunction, high blood pressure, heart disease, brain damage (affecting memory and concentration, for example) and stomach problems.

Psychological symptoms include depression (the most common), anxiety, phobias, paranoia and jealousy, a maudlin outlook and anger, sometimes accompanied by violent and uncontrollable rages.

Keeping your independence

'I've been involved with a lovely man for over five years now,' says a divorced mother of a girl and a boy. 'He is a single parent to his son, and his son and I don't get on all that well, but that's not what's stopping me from setting up home with him. I've managed on my own with the children now for years, I have a demanding job, the children's visits to my ex go well – and I just don't want to rock the boat. I can see my friends when I wish, I can do what I like with my money. I love to see my man at weekends and have the occasional holiday with him . . . but that's enough for me. Unfortunately, it's not enough for him, he wants us to buy a place together and make one big happy family. He thinks it will all work out. But I'm not so sure. I've worked hard for the peace that I now have . . . and I don't want to find myself in a divorce situation ever again. I just don't want to take that risk, either for myself or for my children.'

Having a new partner does not necessarily mean that you will inevitably wish to embark upon a second marriage, although many do. Second marriages are, the statistics show, more likely to fail than first marriages. Living in a stepfamily presents new challenges for both parents and children. Recent research shows that some children, particularly girls, do very well in single-parent families when the mother is the lone parent. These children may present problems, should this parent remarry. The main point to consider, for your children, is that a new family will require a considerable period of adjustment and, as with other situations already discussed, children need preparation, support, understanding and time if they are to come to terms with and enjoy a new family life.

9 Four parents . . . and more

'How can I explain to my young teenage daughter that it's all right for me to have my boyfriend to stay, but it's not for her? There are many more problems to divorce – which go on for years – than at first meet the eye.'

There are about six million people, out of a total population of nearly sixty million, living in stepfamilies in Great Britain, according to the National Stepfamily Association. One in three marriages is a remarriage for at least one of the partners. One in four children under the age of sixteen in the UK will experience the divorce of their parents. In the USA half of all children will have to suffer this trauma. Many children experience not only the breakup of their natural parents' marriage, but also the breakup of further marriages as each of their natural parents remarries and subsequently divorces. Such multiple disruptions to their home life have been shown to affect some children badly in different areas of their life.

Single-parent families include not only those where the mother has never married or lived with a partner but also those families made single by separation and divorce. Although not all separated or divorced parents re-partner, a significant proportion will form a stepfamily, either as a result of cohabitation or remarriage. Children are likely to live in single-parent families for some time, perhaps years, before their resident parent remarries and forms a stepfamily. More men than women remarry, but curiously more women with children than women without children remarry, so it appears that it is not the fact of having dependent children at home that militates against remarriage. The younger the children are at the time of their parents' divorce, the more likely they are to acquire step-parents. Many more families are composed of the natural parent, the children and a new partner in cohabitation with the divorced or separated parent. The cohabiting partner may assume the role and responsibilities of a parent, in all but a legal sense.

Is it really for the best?

'He needs a father figure in the house – he's getting out of hand.' Some mothers of sons, like this one, find their children's aggressiveness difficult to cope with and do not appreciate that the aggressive behaviour, in part caused by the loss of a parent, will not be curbed by a so-called substitute father. If anything, a strict stepfather figure is likely to increase aggressive behaviour in the child.

This is just one of the misconceptions surrounding remarriage. Many people believe they are acting in the children's best interests, or they seek to justify their actions as being in their children's interests, whereas in fact they are doing what they themselves want to do. Remarriage can pose problems for both parents and children but, as with parental separation, remarriage can seem very positive for the adult involved, whereas children may find the prospect of a new parental figure more daunting.

Many children would prefer their parents not to remarry, partly because a new marriage more or less confirms the fact that their natural parents will not reunite and partly because they resent what they see as the intrusion upon their parent's time and attention – time that would otherwise have been sent with them – as the following two quotations illustrate.

'Mum was certainly more interested in me and more fun to be with before he came along. She's quite happy now when I go out at weekends and come back late – before he was here, she wouldn't have stood for it.'

'Dad got a girlfriend and we liked her to start with, but after they got married it was different. She kept trying to make us go to bed early and she kept telling us off at meal times. I suppose he would be lonely without her, but it would be better for us if she wasn't there.'

This woman endorses the view that remarriage might not be for the best: 'My first husband left when the children were very small, and I found things very difficult, very tiring, and I was always broke. I've now remarried, and things are easier financially, but there are other problems. He has three children who come to visit every other weekend, which means that there are seven to cook for and look after. After their weekends I'm totally exhausted. His eldest squabbles all the time with my eldest – and his twins gang up on my daughter. I found them burying her in the garden the other day . . . I went crazy. Life would be a lot quieter if I were on my own again with my two.'

The right reasons

Because the advent of a step-parent does not necessarily guarantee the happiness for your children that it may do for you, it is important to think long and hard about your reasons for the marriage. The new family group will, undoubtedly, encounter problems as they learn to live together. Having already encountered family problems, it is especially important to think about how the future could work and to think about some of the more obvious causes of difficulty.

- Do you believe that you are genuinely compatible with your prospective new partner?

- Is your partner compatible with each of your children?

- Do you sincerely believe that the marriage will last this time?

- Do you feel that the relationship is sufficiently solid to withstand the problems that will inevitably arise?

- Do you have real feelings for this person – or are you contemplating marriage simply in order to be part of a couple again and to have greater financial security?

Many of the issues raised in the preceding chapter apply if not more, to this new situation. It is important tha. relationship is sufficiently sound to enable you to resolve conflicts and difficulties together as a team. Some children ma exploit any weaknesses in a relationship as a way of expressing their feelings of insecurity and loss. Children, aware that a new partner will change things for them in the family, may react to the real or imagined threat by being especially difficult and awkward to manage because they feel insecure. It is almost impossible to know at the beginning of the relationship whether or not it will work out, so it is helpful to the children concerned not to rush into a new relationship.

Other people's children

'Other people's children are ghastly,' declared one divorced man with two children of his own, without a thought for his new wife who was apparently meant to accept his two as her own. People without children of their own may find it even harder to become step-parents than those who already have their own children. They may possess little insight into how demanding and how tiring children can be and, of course, they will not have the same bond with the children as the natural parent. They will be expected by those around them to play a role for which they have no experience and, perhaps, little inclination. In addition, the child-free partner may experience considerable resistance when she/he wishes to have children of the new marriage. How will the existing children react? Will they get on?

This is one woman's experience: 'When I met my husband, he was divorced with two children. I recall a friend of mine asking me at the time what I thought of his children. I replied that as far as I could see I would be having all the fun with them but I wouldn't have to do their washing! Things, of course, were not that simple, as I was to discover. Their mother became jealous of me and was endlessly causing mischief. My husband and I had quite different attitudes to what constituted reasonable behaviour – and bed time – for the children. The children's stepfather was dour, rude, to me, although *I* had never done him any harm. I could tell that he couldn't stand the sight of my husband and disliked him turning up to collect the children for a visit. The whole thing was ghastly. I managed for ten years, but believe me I don't have any regrets about our marriage breaking down. I can't tell you what his children thought about it – I don't know.'

Many children become very attached to their step-parents, and they to them. It is important for successful step-relationships that no one tries to be someone that they are not. A stepmother cannot be the natural mother, and a stepfather, equally, cannot easily assume the role of the natural father. Step-relationships are intrinsically different. They can be enriching and fulfilling for everyone concerned, but no step-parent can replace the natural parent in the child's heart. For this reason discipline is often best left to the natural parent: many children will resent a new authority figure in the form of a step-parent. Many children tolerate their step-parents without necessarily liking them. They acknowledge the fact that they are there, but many would not lament their departure.

'Everything was fine while I was playing with them, giving them things, making their life more fun than it had been before, and so on,' says a stepmother of two youngsters, 'but as soon as I tried to stop them eating with their hands at the table – and I'm talking about a twelve-year-old now – I could feel the hostility.'

You may well conclude, as did the woman quoted at the end of the preceding chapter, that tranquillity – achieved after a good deal of reorganization, adjustment and acceptance – is too precious a state to risk. Part-time cohabitation sometimes works better than a second marriage, both for the natural parent and for the children.

Is it all that bad?

This chapter has deliberately painted a gloomy picture of the sorts of problems and feelings likely to beset a second marriage. Second marriages are, statistically speaking, more frail than first marriages and, in order for them to succeed, both partners need to be realistic, thoughtful and sensitive to the needs of the children involved. Even those children who are apparently delighted by the news of the marriage of one of their parents may be harbouring ambivalent attitudes. Being aware of their secret reservations is one way in which you can help your children and increase your chances of a successful second marriage.

Telling the children

Once you have considered all the aspects and interests that you need to take into account when you are making the decision to remarry and have decided to go ahead, you will want to give some thought about how and when to tell your children. It is best that this is done as gradually and in as low-key a manner as possible. Don't be beguiled into thinking that marriage is what the children want for you both, even if they come right out and ask if you are going to get married. They may be asking because they want to know what is going to happen, not because they want it to happen. It is wise to tell your former partner before you tell the children, so that she/he is prepared for the children's reactions and questions.

Explain to the children than you are very fond of this person and that you would like her/him to come and live with you all. The questions will probably start there and you can gradually tell them the news. If you are the children's absent parent, this news will not impose such a very great lifestyle change upon them. They may be genuinely pleased for you, as they may have believed you to be lonely with no one to look after you until now. As the children's resident parent, clearly your marriage is going to have a far greater impact upon your children's life. Their new step-parent will be there in their home all the time. Day-to-day decisions about the home will now more likely be taken by both of you together. Whereas before the children could quite easily have you to themselves, if they wished it, now they will have to compete for your attention. They may well be jealous and may feel shut out. If your children seem put out, angry, withdrawn, detached or out of sorts, do bear in mind how momentous your decision is for them. Even their family position may change: they may no longer, for example, be the eldest child or the youngest child.

Not always the children

'I was living with my son, having left my husband. I fell in love with what I thought was a wonderful man and after many, many visits and weekends and so on, which went well, he moved in with us. We intended to marry after our divorces had come through. We never actually got to that stage because of how he was with my thirteen-year-old son. He was literally jealous – it was absurd. My son did everything he could to make him feel welcome, but this man clearly needed a lot of attention himself. He had left his second wife nearly a year earlier, and he also had children by his first wife and they used to come and visit us. I think he just had too much on his mind – he simply could not cope with two more relationships, the one with me and the other with my son. He lived with us only a few months before we realized it was hopeless and he left.'

This woman's failed relationship, which could have been a second failed marriage, illustrates the fact that it is not only the children who have emotional needs. A partner in a second marriage needs to be alive to the strong bond that exists between natural parent and child and to be aware that in many senses she/he will always come second to the children. Are you psychologically strong enough to take that? Is the relationship strong enough to withstand that reservation? What happens when your own children come to visit? Will each partner of the second marriage will be able to treat all the children equally and with the kindness and consideration that they deserve?

Do remember that children bring about neither the divorce of their parents nor the remarriage of one of their parents to someone else. Children have to live with the decisions adults make about their lives. They are, and they may feel this acutely, powerless to determine their own lives. This sense of lack of control over their lives, particularly in children over the age of ten or eleven, may reveal itself as apathy, laziness, insolence, anger or outright aggressiveness, as they seek to take power in other ways.

The situation can be improved only by showing that you understand. Chastising the children for outward signs of unhappiness can only make things worse. You and your partner will need endless patience, especially during the first and second years of your relationship as all of you adjust. After a couple of years, things will probably improve. Remember, too, that the sooner you embark upon a new relationship after the breakdown of your marriage to the children's other natural parent, the more difficult it may be for your children to adjust to an entirely new set of circumstances in their family home. They will need time to come to terms with each emotional upheaval in their life, although it may not always be possible to arrange this. Ideally, children need a minimum of two years and, preferably, four or five years, after the departure of one of their parents before the advent of a step-parent. It helps to remind ourselves frequently how very great a psychological upheaval it is for children to lose a parent from their day-to-day life. Your children may still feel guilty about the departure of their parent, anger at being abandoned, despair and overwhelming sadness.

Pleasing everyone?

Once one or both of the children's natural parents remarry, or start cohabiting, everyone concerned has to accommodate to new relationships:

- Will the mother's children like their new stepfather? Many children feel that loving a step-parent is a betrayal of their absent parent.

- How will the stepfather get on with the children's natural father when he comes to collect them for a visit?

- How will the stepfather treat the children – as a friend, as an uncle, as a substitute father?

- Will the father's children welcome their new stepmother?

- How will the children's mother respond to her ex-husband's new wife?

- Given that women are expected to play a nurturing role more than men are, will the new stepmother treat the children as her own – or will she be able to adopt a more detached role?

▨ When the new stepfather's own children come to visit, how will they get on with his new wife's children? Will they be jealous of them? Will they question why he left them, only then to become a quasi-father to someone else's children?

▨ When the stepmother already has children of her own, how will her new husband's children feel about them? Will they feel excluded? What will her own children make of these 'new' visiting children?

▨ How many sets of grandparents are the children meant to have feelings for? Are they expected to join in visits to Dad's parents, Mum's parents, their stepmother's parents and their stepfather's parents? A new partner will usually mean that a fresh set of grandparents will become part of the child's life and this can be confusing at first. The children will probably find it easier than you do, however, to accept the idea of eight grandparents: they know that everyone has parents.

It is at times like Christmas, birthdays and special family occasions, such as weddings and christenings, that the complexity of new family relationships can surface, as the following quotations illustrate.

'My husband had been married before and he had two children by that marriage. We had a daughter between us, and, honestly, I longed for a proper family Christmas just between the three of us. But every Christmas I had to pack everything up and the three of us would take off to his first wife's house. Her mother would be there and so would mine. I don't think anyone particularly enjoyed it, but he was determined to have Christmas with all of his children.'

'My parents never spoke to one another after their divorce, so when I was planning my wedding, I decided to invite my mother to the ceremony and my father to the reception afterwards. I thought that was fair and it seemed best to me, but in fact *both* of them were upset.'

'My parents lived close by, so I used to spend Christmas morning with Mum and Christmas evening with Dad. He had remarried, so it was all right for him. But I hated leaving Mum on her own for the rest of Christmas Day: she looked so alone.'

'My in-laws wanted all of us to have Christmas together, but this was impossible to manage because my husband's first wife invariably had the children with her over Christmas. All we could do for my mother- and father-in-law was to have them to stay the week before Christmas, when my husband's children would be there, and celebrate a week early. But it wasn't the same. On top of that it meant that on Christmas Day itself my husband would be celebrating Christmas not only without his children, but with my mother and my brother's children. I used to feel that it was terribly poignant that he should have to join in games and so on with his niece and nephew, while what he really wanted was his two sons. At times he would look desperate, bereft. I wouldn't wish this situation on anyone.'

Finally, here is the sad experience of a woman who formed a close relationship with her stepchildren, only to lose them: 'You don't have any status as such as a stepmother. I had had two stepsons for ten years – so I had seen them grow from small children into teenagers – but, after my marriage to their father collapsed, I never saw them again. I used to dream about them, even four years after my husband had walked out. I used to wonder what they were doing, what they looked like, would I recognize them if I bumped into them in the street? Obviously I had grown very attached to them over the years, although of course we had our ups and downs, just like any family. I did not want to make contact with them because that would have meant going through their mother and I didn't want to be interrogated by her about the breakdown of my marriage – she would certainly have been inquisitive. So I never saw them again. Three years after my husband left I wrote to them at his new address, but they didn't reply. Three years is a long time in a teenager's life. I wonder now if they ever had any attachment, any feelings, for me at all. I expect they're busy with their own lives.'

How do children fare in their parents' second marriages?

The Exeter Family Study showed that remarriage may not always be better for the children. Contrary to popular belief, children in stepfamilies do not necessarily benefit from having two parents in the home. Although they were financially better off, they seemed to experience much the same risk of problems as children with single parents. In some areas, such as health, children had even more problems in stepfamilies, possibly as a result of adjusting to a new parent.

Compared with intact families, psychosomatic health problems were twice as likely to affect children from single-parent families, but children from stepfamilies were six times as likely to suffer this type of illness. Reports that their behaviour upset others were twice as likely to come from single-parent children, but stepchildren were ten times as likely to report it, and their parents confirmed that their behaviour was causing problems.

It is when the children are subjected to successive breakups that the research findings become even starker. The Exeter Family Study found that children living in multiply disrupted families on average had many more problems in the areas measured than any other type of family.

It appears, then, that the children's health and education are both adversely affected. These findings have been borne out in a number of other studies in the USA and in Great Britain and confirm that separation and divorce, and remarriage, can have short- and long-term negative influences on children.

American sociologist Amitai Etzioni explains in the book *The Spirit of Community* that a child's two natural parents living together make up a mutually supportive 'education coalition'. The parents play different, complementary, even contradictory roles. One parent may stress the need for achievement while the other balances it by underlining the need, for example, for some exercise in the fresh air. One parent may encourage the child to take intellectual risks with homework, while the other, more cautiously, suggests that the teacher's guidelines should be adhered to. The parents discuss with each other their child's achievements, progress and problems with a sense of the child's overall educational attainment in mind. But, as Etzioni writes:

> The sequence of divorce followed by a succession of boy or girlfriends, a second marriage, and frequently another divorce and another

turnover of partners often means a repeatedly disrupted educational coalition. Each change in participants involves a change in the educational agenda for the child. Each partner cannot be expected to pick up the previous one's education post and program . . . As a result, changes in parenting partners mean, at best, a deep disruption in a child's education, though of course several disruptions cut deeper into the effectiveness of the education coalition than just one.

Helping the child with schoolwork

In some cases neither natural parents nor step-parents participate in their children's education at all. However, most children will benefit if their parents – either natural or step – become involved and supportive. This is another important way of showing children that you care, provided that you help in a supportive way rather than a criticizing or censorious manner. Show that you are genuinely interested by asking them how many homework subjects they have each night, what they are and how you can help.

When it comes to parent-teacher meetings and other school events and activities, step-parents may best be guided by the feelings of their partners and their stepchildren as to whether or not they should attend. Some children like all four parents to attend, while others would find this embarrassing, believing that it singles them out as 'different'.

'My son didn't want all of us to attend to start with,' says one father, 'but he told one of his schoolfriends about it and she said, "Why not? I like all mine turning up!" Thus reassured, he changed his mind and the four of us went . . . with no problems at all.'

Name changes

The question of changing names is a peculiarly fraught area, which needs to be discussed if and when the children's mother remarries. Should she take her new husband's name, with the result that she has a different surname from that of her children, or should both she and the children change their name? Should all of them retain their current name, which, for the children, will have been their name since their birth? Whatever the decision, it has to be a compromise. The children's natural father may dislike the idea of his children taking the surname of their stepfather, and he may want to be consulted about plans to alter his children's surname.

Parents and children often work out what suits them best and need encouragement to do so. Small children can find a change of surname very confusing, but parents can discuss this with their children and new partner.

It may not be appropriate to expect the children, whatever their age, to call their step-parent Mum or Dad. They may prefer to acknowledge the fact that their relationship to the step-parent is different by calling them by their first name.

Here are two experiences of the name problem in stepfamilies:

'I used to call my stepfather Dad, until I realized that he wasn't my real father, but now I call him by his proper name.'

'I recall receiving a card from my stepsons on Mother's Day . . . and feeling rather disturbed by it. I wasn't their mother, although I was very attached to them.'

A new baby

There can be no question about the fact that the arrival of a new baby will impose new strains on the stepfamily. A baby imposes stresses on any parental relationship, and these are likely to be more marked in stepfamilies. What will the mother's existing children make of the baby? What will the child who until now has been the youngest make of this new arrival, now that he or she is no longer in that position? How will the children, who may still be feeling a sense of abandonment from the loss of one parent, respond to that parent now having a new baby to capture his interest? Will they feel left out, superfluous, jealous?

'I couldn't believe that my father and his girlfriend were going to have a baby . . . at *his* age – he's fifty this year!' was one eighteen-year-old's response. 'I'm off to university, so I shan't see all that much of him in any case. I don't reckon he'll stick it out, he'll probably bunk off like he did with us.'

The new parent's previous partner may well also feel jealous or unhappy about the birth of a child as compelling evidence of intimacy with new partner.

All these problems can be improved upon by open and honest discussion. Don't let your children find out about important events such as the expected birth of a baby by accident: tell them. Don't let your partner find out through mutual friends, let her/him know. Open communication is the best way to resolve conflicts, resentment, jealousy and anger.

The arrival of a baby is a special challenge in a stepfamily or in a family that has already seen successive disruptions and change. Be happy, but be aware that this new baby may carry a different significance for your children and for your previous partner from that which it carries for you. Both new parents need to make sure that all the children in the family are included in welcoming the baby, and older children, in particular, may need special reassurance that they remain as important in the family as the new arrival, or they may be profoundly hurt.

The children growing up

Many adults in stepfamilies observe the problems of adolescence in their older children and stepchildren and feel that they must be to blame for their children's attitudes and behaviour. Understandably, they often overlook the fact that teenagers need to challenge parental authority; refusal to communicate, moodiness, insolent and inconsiderate behaviour, peculiar dress and hairstyles, lethargy, depression and anxiety are all quite normal elements of adolescence. These sometimes alarming traits are frequently seen in most teenagers and are experienced by all parents whatever their family circumstances, irrespective of whether or not divorce is a feature. Parental separation cannot be held to account for all the problems that parents typically experience with teenagers: it can help step-parents, when problems seem overwhelming, to remind themselves that some of their difficulties are universally experienced by most families.

The normal problems of adolescence are inevitably overlaid with the problems caused by parental separation. Teenagers find themselves subject to two different sets of rules in their two homes, just at the time when they are challenging parental authority. Many teenagers find it difficult to combine their social activities with their weekend visits to their non-resident parents. Some may resent the intrusion into their weekends, caused by pre-arranged visits, at a time when most children elect to spend most of their time with their friends. Neither parent nor step-parent should take it personally when they observe that their teenage child is starting to break away, and is beginning to challenge the long-established routine for visits to the absent parent and to show that they want to be with friends of their own age. All this kind of behaviour is a perfectly normal part of adolescent development: it does not mean that the child no longer wishes to have contact with the parent or step-parent.

Your personal life

Many children find the idea of one of their parents being sexually active with a new partner disgusting. Many children believe that their parents are too old 'for that'. It will help your children to accept your new relationship if you appreciate this and refrain from overtly sexual behaviour in front of them.

Child abuse

Parents and step-parents should be alert to the possibility of sexual attraction between step-siblings and between stepchild and step-parent, most commonly between a stepfather and stepdaughter. It may help to guard against the dangers of such relationships by following specific rules about clothing and by making sure, for example, that everyone has a right to privacy in the bathroom. It is best that everyone is properly dressed in the home and that the bathroom is not shared.

Incest and child abuse are much more common, and always have been so, than many people believe. Children from disrupted families are at much higher risk of physical abuse than children from intact families. Research has shown that stepfamilies may be especially susceptible to the development of incestuous relationships and that children may be more likely to be exposed to sexual abuse. Parents need to be responsible for protecting their children from such dangers.

Being realistic

For a second marriage to work, both partners need to be realistic and sensitive to the feelings of children and former partners. Second marriages can too easily crumple under the weight of hostility from friends, relatives and, especially, from former spouses and partners, as well as from the children in the family. Assuming responsibility for someone else's children is an enormous task and this should be acknowledged. Be realistic in your expectations: neither expect nor give instant love, for this is not credible. Allow yourself and your stepchildren to take things at a steady pace. If they seem unhappy or miserable, try to talk to them gently about why this might be and establish what you can do to help them. Don't just hope that their mood will pass eventually: actively support them and show them that you care.

Your children and stepchildren should at all times be treated with the love, respect and warmth that indicates to them that they are very special to you and that they can always rely on you to be supportive.

SOME GUIDELINES FOR STEP-PARENTS

- Be clear, explicit and consistent about house rules: decide what is important in this respect and what is not, and keep to your decision.

- Don't attribute all problems to living in a stepfamily. Intact families have their problems, too.

- Refrain from burdening the children with money worries – which they cannot help with in any case.

- Bear in mind that many children fear a second separation and that they will take rows between you and your partner more seriously, perhaps, than you yourselves do.

This chapter may seem somewhat negative, but being aware of the problems and of the need to support each other to overcome them can mean that stepfamilies can be every bit as rewarding and enriching for each member as other types of families. So, allow yourself to rejoice in your new-found family. Each of you can benefit by this new association.

0 The children grow up

'When my husband and I argue, our son attempts to distract us. He's only three and a half, but you can already see that it distresses him. So, whenever I'm thinking divorceful thoughts, which I do quite often, I look at him and think again.'

There has been a very profound change in our attitudes to marriage in the last thirty years. Marriages based on a clear division of male and female roles, as they were in the past, are known to be more stable than marriages in which love, attraction and shared activities are the prerequisites. What happens when love gives way to companionship and attraction fades in favour of someone else? People no longer, in general, believe that they have a responsibility to maintain the marriage for the sake of the children. It has been believed for years that it is better for the children to terminate a poor marriage than to continue suffering. But most of the evidence suggests otherwise.

Dr Sebastian Kraemer has observed that there is a collective wish not to look at children's pain and that we can hardly bear to think about it because, if we did, we would have to have a social revolution in our attitudes to parenting and marriage. Dr Kraemer believes that if it was part of our culture to acknowledge that divorce hurts children, it is just possible, with greater wisdom and under-standing about the stresses both of family life and of divorce, that couples might stay together if they realized what they were doing by separating.

Children are devalued and diminished in many ways, by the separation of their parents. Their sense of identity is shaken, and their self-confidence is severely affected.

Little research has been done in Great Britain on children living in stepfamilies, but work carried out in the USA shows that stepfamilies pose a range of problems for both parents and children. Parents will be able to overcome some of these themselves, while others will require help from outside. Stepfamilies suffer from the pressure of feeling that they need to mould themselves on an original two-parent family, instead of accepting that for the children, however much they grow to love their step-parent, they can never replace the children's natural parent. Some children may never settle into a new family way of life, and can remain miserable and difficult. They may still hope that their parents will reunite. The children's unhappiness may show itself in minor or major ways, which may settle down over time. Even when parents do not remarry, children can take quite a long time to adjust to the family breakup, and some never fully adjust.

At worst stepfamilies can disrupt established loyalties, create uncertainties, provoke profound anxieties and not only damage the children's emotional security but, in some cases, imperil their physical safety as well.

For a child the loss of a parent is an overwhelming trauma, which you cannot 'make better' by forming a stepfamily. Many children do not believe that they are happier or better off in their new family, whether it be a single-parent family or stepfamily. They yearn for what is lost. Their psychological disturbance may be manifested in a variety of ways: aggressive behaviour, stomach upsets, being withdrawn and moody, losing their friends, bedwetting, school phobia, lying, stealing and fighting, for example.

The majority of children accept their parents' divorce within two to three years. The consequences for children of divorcing parents are, naturally, not all the same. Many children eventually do well, although the scars may remain. Even children of the same family may be differently affected, with one child seriously disturbed and another not at all – or even benefiting. The eventual outcome for children depends to some extent not only on what has been lost but also on what has been created in its place. If, after the divorce, the children experience life in a happy family and there is an absence of conflict in that family and between their two natural parents, they are likely to fare better.

The Exeter Family Study concludes:

Although *most* children do not exhibit acute difficulties beyond the initial stage of family breakdown a *significant minority* of children encounter long-term problems . . . [These children] were more likely to report problems in key areas of their lives, including psychosomatic disorders, difficulties with school work and a low sense of self-esteem. They were more likely to feel confused and uninvolved in arrangements about their future and to have lasting feelings of concern about both their resident and non-resident parents. Parental conflict and financial difficulties are clearly important features of family reorganization that are associated with adverse outcomes for children. However, in this study it appeared that a more important adverse factor was the loss of a parent and the consequences, which included the risk that history would repeat itself with the breakdown of subsequent parental relationships.

Dr M.P.M. Richards, director of the Centre for Family Research at Cambridge University, speaking at the annual meeting of the British Psychological Society in April 1995 at Warwick University in the UK, noted that the children of divorced parents suffer economic and social consequences that may adversely affect the rest of their life.

Dr Richards's work is based on data collected for the 1958 Birth Study, which contains information on 17,000 children. In line with results from other such studies, these data show that there are long-term disadvantages for children associated with parental separation and/or divorce. Children of divorced parents are likely to suffer increased poverty, do far less well at school, marry earlier and suffer higher rates of divorce themselves. Girls tended to marry earlier, with a 45 per cent chance of marrying by the age of twenty, compared with a 15 per cent chance for those whose parents stayed together. Boys showed a similar pattern, with 16 per cent marrying before the age of twenty, compared with 5 per cent of those from intact families.

Dr Richards said at the time: 'There's something very specific and special about divorce. The children's self-esteem tends to fall. If there is no father to support the household, this is seen as a judgement on their self-worth. The children have to face the fact that their father appears not to want to see them.'

Professor Mike Wadsworth, director of the Medical Research Council National Survey of Health and Development, has (in publications dating back over the last ten years and, using data from the 1958 National Child Development Study) emphasized the long-term disadvantage to children who have experienced parental separation and/or divorce. He is especially concerned about the effects of failure at school on future work opportunities.

It is thought that half of all fathers completely lose contact with their children within two years of their divorce. They are more likely to do so if the mother remarries. Remarriage of either parent can, of course, influence contact arrangements, but do not usually disturb well-established routines.

The earlier the parental separation takes place in the child's life, the worse it is likely to be for the child. Contact with the absent parent is more likely to be broken, and it is more likely that the mother, who is usually the resident parent, will remarry. In the event of early parental separation, it is more difficult for the non-resident parent to maintain a close, long-lasting relationship with the child, and it is more likely that both parents will remarry, and perhaps have a second family, thereby creating a new set of circumstances for the child.

A 1988 study by American researchers J.S. Wallerstein, S.B. Corbin and J.M. Lewis found that the after-effects of divorce persisted for many years. At this ten-year follow-up, some of the young people they had first seen in 1978 as a group of children who were undergoing their parents' divorce were burdened with vivid memories of the stressful events surrounding the divorce and admitted that they felt apprehensive about repeating their parents' unhappy marriage and consequent divorce during their own adulthood. The authors of this study believe that the long-term effects upon the children were not so much due to the divorce as to the disrupted parenting and diminished quality of life that often follows parental separation.

Work on the data already examined by Dr Richards (mentioned above), which was carried out by Kathleen Kiernan in 1992, shows similar trends to those reported by Dr Richards. She found that young people who have lived in a single-parent family, headed by the mother, before they are sixteen years old as a result of divorce, are more likely to leave school at the minimum age and to leave home by the age of eighteen compared with those in intact families. The chances of those events occurring among children who become part of a stepfamily following divorce are also significantly greater when compared with those in intact families.

These are just some of the studies to have been published in the last ten years that confirm what many people have suspected: namely, that children caught in the middle of a parental separation or divorce inevitably suffer, both in the short term, when their problems, can be acute, and in the long term when their life chances may be diminished.

Self-image

Children may be devalued by divorce. Their sense of identity or development of positive identity, is gained through testing and relating to both parents day by day in different situations. How a child's parents react and respond to the child determines the child's view of herself. Children of separated parents may continue to feel rejected by the absent parent no matter how good the contact arrangements are. Feelings of rejection, which may have been triggered by the departure of the parent from the home, can take a long time to heal, even when there are good contact arrangements with the absent parent. When there is little continuing support from the absent parent, those feelings may never subside.

Friendships

Because children often feel diminished and embarrassed by parental separation and feel miserable, their friendships may suffer and they may find it more difficult than happier children to maintain their friendships and to make new ones, especially if they have to move to a new neighbourhood and new school. Children whose parents have divorced are more likely to choose friends who have been in the same situation.

Relationships

As we have already seen, both girls and boys are more likely to leave home and to marry earlier than their peers in intact families. They are also more likely to be promiscuous. Girls are more likely than their contemporaries from intact families to show early heterosexual behaviour and attention-seeking behaviour towards males. Women who have experienced the breakdown of their parents' marriage are three times more likely to cohabit in their teens than those women who have been brought up by their natural parents. These women are also more likely to become pregnant during their teenage years.

Marriage

Many young people fear repeating their parents' mistakes. Women who grew up in stepfamilies formed after divorce are significantly more likely to have married before the age of twenty. The odds of a girl brought up in a stepfamily marrying in her teens are 3.6 times greater than those of a woman from an intact family. Women from other family situations are no more likely to be married than their contemporaries who have grown up with both natural parents.

Men from stepfamilies that have resulted from marital breakdown are more likely than their peers to cohabit, and to marry before the age of twenty-one.

Career prospects

About half of single-parent families live on state benefits, and studies show that this economic disadvantage to the children of the family persists into adulthood. Children of some divorced parents tend to be less well-educated and, consequently, to take lower paid jobs, to lack a sense of direction about their future, to achieve less well than their natural fathers and to be in less prestigious occupations than their contemporaries brought up by both parents. Reduced financial resources, as well as feelings of insecurity and lack of confidence, are believed to be to blame for these bleak trends.

Did they realize?

The Exeter Family Study found that many parents, when asked about their expectations and experience of life after divorce, said that they had not been fully aware of what the consequences of separation might be for themselves or for their children. Many of them felt that life was improved by the ending of a failed relationship; but it was also clear that their children often regarded any improvement in a much less positive light. In fact, parents' own health and sense of wellbeing can suffer as a result of divorce, and some researchers have suggested that this contributes to a reduced ability to parent responsibility and well at that time. The children who took part in the Exeter Family Study are not yet grown up, and it will, therefore, be some years before we may observe how they have made the transition from childhood to adulthood. It remains to be seen whether or not they will encounter some of the long-term disadvantages encountered by those who grew up in separated families, which other studies have found to exist.

It could be said that parental separation and consequent divorce during the last twenty to thirty years have constituted a massive social experiment, the results of which are only now becoming widely apparent. Many people regret their divorce: over half of men and nearly a third of women believe that it would have been better to continue with the marriage. Even more children regret their parents' divorce, and they continue to do so, sometimes for the rest of their lives.

It is difficult to imagine how anyone who is familiar with the research on the subject of children and divorce can continue to believe that divorce could be a positive event for children. The weight of evidence is decisively against it. Many children come through the initial pain and deprivation within two years, but a significant minority do not. When parents are able to work together to remain supportive to their children, after the initial stages are over, children can begin to adapt to and accept their changed circumstances. This can, in some cases, take a long time. In less favourable circumstances, children will find it harder to adjust, particularly if hostility between their mother and father continues to disrupt their lives. While it is recognized that it is not always possible for parents to stay together, and not always wise to do so when there is violence and abuse in the family, the scale of the problem is growing. One in three British children, and one in two in the USA, grow up with limited access to one of their parents.

This is a huge problem: one in three British children will experience parental divorce before the age of sixteen and one in two American children will suffer in the same way. Now that we know so much more about the emotional pain and the long-term psychological and material disadvantages suffered by children who have endured parental divorce, we must do much more to put the interests of the children first and foremost. We must become far more finely attuned to our children's needs and better informed about the potential for psychological and material deprivation in the lives of children caught in the middle.

Further reading

Books

Bowlby, J., *Attachment and Loss*, vol. 1: *Attachment* (Penguin Books, London, 1991).

Burrett, J., *To & Fro Children* (Thorsons, London, 1993).

Cockett, M., and Tripp, J., *The Exeter Family Study. Family Breakdown and Its Impact upon Children* (University of Exeter Press, Exeter, November 1994).

Dench, G., *The Frog, The Prince & The Problem of Men* (Neanderthal Books, London, 1994).

Etzioni, A., *The Spirit of Community* (Fontana Press, London, 1995).

Itzin, C., *Splitting Up: Single Parent Liberation* (Virago, London, 1980).

Mitchell, A., *Children in the Middle* (Tavistock Publications, London, 1985).

Pasley, K., and Ihinger-Tallman, M., *Remarriage & Stepparenting* (Guildford Press, New York and London, 1987).

Schaffer, H. R., *Making Decisions about Children* (Basil Blackwell, Oxford, 1990).

Shackleton, F., and Timbs, O., *The Divorce Handbook* (Thorsons, London, 1992).

Stone, L., *Road to Divorce* (Oxford University Press, Oxford, 1995).

Wadsworth, M.E.J., *The Imprint of Time. Childhood History and Adult Life* (Clarendon Press, Oxford, 1991).

Wallerstein, J.S., and Kelly, J.B., *Surviving the Breakup:How Children and Parents Cope with Divorce* (Grant McIntyre, London, 1980).

Wells, R., *Helping Children Cope with Divorce* (Sheldon Press, London, 1993).

Wells, R., *Helping Children Cope with Grief* (Sheldon Press, London, 1995).

Journals, booklets and chapters

The Children Act 1989 – An Introductory Guide for the NHS (Health Publications, Heywood, Lancs, November 1991).

Cockett, M., Kuh, D., and Tripp, J., 'The Needs of Disturbed Adolescents', *Children and Society* 2, 93–113, 1987.

Cox, K., and Desforges, M., *Children and Divorce: A Guide for Adults* (available from Kathleen Cox, 6 Whinfell Court, Sheffield S11 9QA; tel. 0114 2350534).

De'Ath, E., *Teenagers Growing Up in a Stepfamily* (National Stepfamily Association, Publication No. 3, 1990).

For the Sake of the Children (transcript of BBC1's *Panorama* special, screened 7 February 1994; issued by BBC News and Current Affairs Publicity, tel. 0181 576 8367).

Kiernan, K.E., 'Teenage Marriage and Marital Breakdown: A Longitudinal Study', *Population Studies* 40, 35–54, 1986.

Kiernan, K.E., 'The Impact of Family Disruption in Childhood on Transitions made in Young Adult Life', *Population Studies* 46, 213–34, 1992.

Kiernan, K.E., and Chase-Landsdale, P.L., *Children and Marital Breakdown: Short and Long Term Consequences*, Proceedings of the European Demographic Conference, Paris, 21–25 October 1991.

National Family Mediation, *Giving Children a Voice in Mediation* (July 1994).

Richards, M.P.M., 'Children, Parents and Families: Developmental Psychology and The Re-ordering of Relationships at Divorce', *International Journal of Law and the Family* 1, 295–317, 1987.

Richards, M.P.M., 'Post-divorce Arrangements for Children: A Psychological Perspective', *Journal of Social Welfare Law* 69, 133–51, 1982.

Utting, D., *Family and parenthood: Supporting families, preventing breakdown: a guide to the debate* (Joseph Rowntree Foundation, York, February 1995).

Wallerstein, J.S., Corbin, S.B., and Lewis, J.M., 'Children of Divorce: A Ten Year Study'. In E.M. Hetherington and J.D. Arasteh (eds), *Impact of Divorce, Single Parenting and Step-parenting on Children*, 198–214 (Lawrence Erlbaum, Hillsdale, USA, 1988).

Whitehead, B.D., 'Dan Quayle Was Right', *Atlantic Monthly*, USA, April 1993.

Useful addresses

UK
Child Support Advice agency
Tel: 0345 133133

Gingerbread
16/17 Clerkenwell Close
London EC1R 0AA
Tel: 0171 336 8183

Grandparents' Federation
General Secretary: Noreen Tingle
Room 3
Moot House
The Stow
Harlow
Essex CM20 3AG
Tel: 01279 444964

Families Need Fathers
134 Curtain Road
London EC2A 3AR
Tel: 0171 613 5060

Family Mediators Association
PO Box 2028
Hove
East Sussex BN3 3HU
Tel: 01273 673544

London Marriage Guidance
Council
76a New Cavendish Street
London W1M 7LB
Tel: 0171 580 1087

National Association of Family
Mediation and Conciliation
Services
9 Tavistock Place
London WC1H 9SN
Tel: 0171 383 5993

National Council for One-Parent
Families
255 Kentish Town Road
London NW5 2LX
Tel: 0171 267 1361

National Stepfamily Association
Chapel House
18 Hatton Place
London EC1N 8RU
Tel: 0171 209 2460

Relate National Marriage
Guidance
Head Office
Herbert Gray College
Little Church Street
Rugby CV21 3AP
Tel: 01788 573241

Social Security advice line
Tel: 0800 666 555

Solicitors Family Law Association
PO Box 302
Orpington
Kent BR6 8QX
Tel: 01689 850227

USA

Academy of Family Mediators
4 Militia Drive
Lexington
MA 02173
Tel: 408 476 9225

American Association for
Counselling & International
Association of Counselling
Services, Inc.
5999 Stevenson Avenue
Alexandria
VA 22304
Tel: 703 820 4700

American Association of Marriage
and Family Counsellors
255 Yale Avenue
Claremont
CA 917711

Association of Family and
Conciliation Courts (AFCC)
329 West Wilson Street
Madison
WI 53703
Tel: 608 251 4001

Divorce Lifeline
1013 Eighth Avenue
Seattle
Washington 98104
Tel: 202 347 2279

Parents without Partners Inc.
7910 Woodmont Avenue
Washington, D.C. 20014
Tel: 202 638 1320

Index